STRANGERS
or
FRIENDS

**Recent Titles in
Contributions in Political Science**
Series Editor: Bernard K. Johnpoll

Ban The Bomb: A History of SANE, the Committee for a Sane Nuclear Policy, 1957–1985
Milton S. Katz

Republicans and Vietnam, 1961–1968
Terry Dietz

The Politics of Developed Socialism: The Soviet Union as a Postindustrial State
Donald P. Kelley

Harry S. Truman: The Man from Independence
William F. Levantrosser, editor

News from Somewhere: Connecting Health and Freedom at the Workplace
Gary A. Lewis

"Pursuing the Just Cause of Their People": A Study of Contemporary Armenian Terrorism
Michael M. Gunter

When Marxists Do Research
Pauline Marie Vaillancourt

Government Violence and Repression: An Agenda for Research
Michael Stohl and George A. Lopez, editors

Rural Public Administration: Problems and Prospects
Jim Seroka, editor

Hidden Power: The Seniority System and Other Customs of Congress
Maurice B. Tobin

The Sino-Indian Border Dispute: A Legal Study
Chih H. Lu

The Primoridal Challenge: Ethnicity in the Contemporary World
John F. Stack, Jr., editor

Strangers or Friends

Principles for a New
Alien Admission Policy

Mark Gibney

Contributions in Political Science, Number 157

GREENWOOD PRESS
New York • Westport, Connecticut • London

Library of Congress Cataloging-in-Publication Data

Gibney, Mark
  Strangers or friends.

  (Contributions in political science, ISSN 0147–1066; no. 157)
  Bibliography: p.
  Includes index.
  1. Emigration and immigration—Government policy.
I. Title. II. Series.
JV6271.G53   1986   350.81'7   86–7572
ISBN 0–313–25344–7 (lib. bdg. : alk. paper)

Copyright © 1986 by Mark Gibney

All rights reserved. No portion of this book may be reproduced, by any process or technique, without the express written consent of the publisher.

Library of Congress Catalog Card Number: 86–7572
ISBN: 0–313–25344–7
ISSN: 0147–1066

First published in 1986

Greenwood Press, Inc.
88 Post Road West, Westport, Connecticut 06881

Printed in the United States of America

∞

The paper used in this book complies with the Permanent Paper Standard issued by the National Information Standards Organization (Z39.48–1984).

10 9 8 7 6 5 4 3 2 1

Copyright Acknowledgments

We gratefully acknowledge permission to reprint extracts from the following sources:

Bruce A. Ackerman, *Social Justice in the Liberal State*. Copyright © 1980 by Yale University Press.

Peter G. Brown and Henry Shue, eds., *Boundaries: National Autonomy and Its Limits* (Totowa, N.J.: Rowman and Littlefield, c1981).

John Rawls, *A Theory of Justice*. Reprinted by permission of Harvard University Press.

Henry Shue, *Basic Rights: Subsistence, Affluence, and U.S. Foreign Policy*. Copyright © 1980 by Princeton University Press.

Contents

Acknowledgments   vii

Introduction   ix

Part I   Theories for Admitting Aliens

Chapter 1	Michael Walzer	3
Chapter 2	John Rawls	23
Chapter 3	Peter Singer and Henry Shue	35
Chapter 4	Bruce Ackerman	47
Chapter 5	Community in America	55

Part II   Developing a New Alien Admission System

Chapter 6	Individual Obligations	71
Chapter 7	The Harm Principle	79
Chapter 8	The Basic Rights Principle	103
Chapter 9	A Chapter of Examples	109

vi   Contents

Chapter 10	Present Policy Compared	139

Concluding Remarks	151
Selected Bibliography	153
Index	163

Acknowledgments

I would like to thank Alex Aleinikoff, Paul Courant, George Grassmuck, and Ernie Wilson for their useful comments on an earlier draft. I am particularly grateful to John Chamberlin for all the help he has given me. Without his great wisdom and efforts this book would not have been possible.

There are other people who have helped me in a less direct manner whom I would also like to thank. I have groups of friends throughout the country whom I treasure, and who are very patient with unannounced visits. Hank Heitowit provided much needed financial support for several summers despite my "70 percent" effort. Michael Blumenthal was very helpful at a critical time merely by waving his foul cigar in front of my face and encouraging me to go on. Finally, I have two professors from my undergraduate days who have been very influential in my life—Charles Serns and Frank Murphy—two outstanding teachers and human beings.

I cannot think of anyone who has been blessed with a more loving family than I have been: from grandparents, aunts, uncles, and cousins, to my brother and two sisters, and their spouses and adorable children. My parents have always thought I could accomplish anything (and everything), and their confidence is quite infectious and appreciated. Saying thank you to them for all they have done for me seems insufficient, and it is. Vanessa and Matt have had to suffer through the writing of this and I would like to thank them for their part, particularly turning down "their music" upon frequent request. Finally, I dedicate this book to Rita, whose love and enthusiasm have aided enormously in helping to carry the day.

Introduction

My aim is to frame an alien admission policy for the United States that will meet certain duties to those who live outside the United States, and, at the same time, maintain the autonomy of the U.S. community and its subcommunities. I have divided this work into two parts. The first is a discussion of how other political philosophers have looked at the question of admitting foreigners, or how their theories might address such matters. The second part of this work attempts to build on this philosophical framework and some of the critiques of these theories that I offer.

The political thought that has dominated in the area of alien admissions has come from some of the great names in international law, names like Hugo Grotius and Emmerich Vattel.[1] Their theories relied on two interconnected concepts: that nations properly demarcated individuals from one another, and that control over national borders was a sovereign right. In addition, there was the added assumption that control over a nation's borders was essential to maintaining this sovereignty. Typical is this statement from Vattel:

Every nation has the right to refuse to admit a foreigner into the country, when he cannot enter without putting the nation in evident danger, or doing it manifest injury . . . it belongs to the nation to judge whether its circumstances will or will not justify the admission of the foreigner.[2]

Some political philosophers have begun to question the view that nations are insulated from one another. For example, Charles Beitz has argued that nations today are much more interdependent, and that national boundaries do not demarcate moral boundaries.[3] Even some who think of themselves as "statists" have recognized similar changes in the international system.[4] Others have pointed out the growing importance of human rights, and the shift from seeing individuals merely as indirect beneficiaries of such rights, to seeing individuals as the center of human rights theory.[5]

Even if the nation-state system itself is not undergoing a process of change, the world itself seems to be. In a well-received piece on immigration issues, Michael Teitelbaum cites International Labour Organization projections that in the next twenty years there will be a need for an additional 600–700 million new jobs in developing countries.[6] Societies that have traditionally sent migrants to the United States (with the exception of Cuba and Jamaica) will see a population increase of 90 percent within this same period. Guestworker programs in Western Europe (and the de facto guestworker program that exists in the United States) have already shown the strengths and weaknesses of admitting foreign citizens for their labor.[7]

Meeting the subsistence needs of millions of individuals is not the only pressing concern. There are approximately thirteen million refugees in the world at the present time. Unless the multitude of unjust regimes somehow change their inhumane ways, we should only expect this phenomenon to grow.

Alien admissions has been a perplexing American public policy problem for quite some time. The cry in Washington now, as in other times in our past, is that we have lost control of our borders. The current stalemate in Congress over the Simpson-Mazzoli legislation is just another indication that something needs to be done.[8] However, there seems to be little agreement (even between those with the same ideological outlook) on what that "something" is.

Introduction xi

I do not profess to know what is needed to solve the alien admission problems of the United States, or of any other country. The contribution that I make here is in asking whether we are addressing the right questions, and employing the correct criteria, under our current alien admission practices. I try to develop a theoretical perspective on alien admissions that purposely removes itself from the nuts and bolts of the current debate. As a result, instead of addressing such questions as employer sanctions, worker identity cards, guestworker provisions, whether married brothers and sisters should have a quota preference, and so on, I go back to square one and ask: (1) on what basis can we, or should we, distinguish between "members" and "strangers," and (2) even if we can make such a distinction, do some strangers have compelling claims for admission to this country?

PART I—THEORIES FOR ADMITTING ALIENS

Chapter 1 is an examination of Michael Walzer's theory of alien admissions. There are two themes of Walzer's that I focus on: community and affinity. By "community" Walzer means a caring and sharing between individuals who not only share a physical space, but who also share a common life together. Walzer believes that for communities to exist there needs to be a sharp distinction drawn between those who are a part of the community (members) and those who are not (strangers). He is also a staunch advocate of the autonomy of communities, and the need to protect this autonomy from incursion by outside nations. Balanced against this members-strangers dichotomy, however, is Walzer's view that there are certain "affinities" with individuals in other lands. These affinities serve as the basis for a Walzerian alien admission policy. I challenge the basis of some of these affinities. I also question Walzer's particular mix of affinities and community.

In Chapter 2 I frame an alien admission system from John Rawls's theory. Although Rawls has not addressed alien admission issues, his discussion of defending the liberties of individuals in other lands naturally lends itself to such a discussion. What naturally emerges is an alien admission system that seeks to protect individual autonomy when that autonomy is seriously threatened. In this chapter I also examine the Brian Barry-Charles Beitz critique of Rawls's theory that argues that individual autonomy is not protected when individuals do not have the means of subsistence. Both Barry and Beitz argue that Rawls's two principles of justice should be extended to the international arena. I accept this position, but I stress that it is essential to distinguish between the proceeds from exploiting the world's resources, and equal access to the world's resources.

Peter Singer and Henry Shue are the focus of Chapter 3. Unlike Walzer and Rawls, Singer and Shue do not work within the confines of the traditional view of the nation-state. Singer's thesis is that if it is possible to prevent something bad from happening without incurring large costs we are morally obligated to do so. The alien admission system that emerges from Singer's theory is one that seeks to aid individuals in other lands who are in serious need.

Henry Shue argues that all individuals possess certain basic rights—subsistence, security, and liberty—that other individuals are morally obligated to meet. Shue also argues that duties can be divided into three types: a duty not to deprive, a duty to protect, and a duty to aid. On one level Shue's notion of basic rights fits in quite nicely with an alien admission system. I argue, however, that Shue's liberty right is not as basic as the right to subsistence and security. I also question Shue's analysis of the right to subsistence. Beyond this, my main critique of Shue's theory is that he is too indeterminate in setting forth who has the duty to protect and the duty to aid.

In Chapter 4 I examine Bruce Ackerman's attempts to frame an alien admission policy. Ackerman's position is that individuals in other countries have a prima facie right to migrate to other lands unless this migration would destroy the "liberal dialogue" in the receiving country. I argue that Ackerman's theory does not go far enough in maintaining and protecting the communal autonomy of the receiving society.

In Chapter 5 I examine the concept of community in this country in the context of alien admissions.

PART II—DEVELOPING A NEW ALIEN ADMISSION SYSTEM

Part II is devoted to framing an alien admission system. In Chapter 6 I argue that individual citizens have duties in the context of international politics; but I also argue that because of the disruption that alien admissions will bring to a receiving society, there is a need to limit individuals from meeting their duties to others through alien admissions. Chapters 7 and 8 are devoted to two principles that lie at the base of the alien admission system that I propose. The seventh chapter is a discussion of the Harm Principle (HP). This principle states that a nation should not harm individuals in other societies, and that there is a special duty to aid those whom we have harmed. Alien admission practices should be an integral part in meeting the special duties that arise under the HP. The eighth chapter examines the Basic Rights Principle (BRP). This principle states that even if one nation has not caused harm to individuals in a particular society, there will still be some duty to aid those in serious need—again, in some instances through alien admissions. The BRP is a weaker principle than the HP, and duties under it are not nearly as far-ranging. I introduce a concept of "Fair Share" that serves as both a coordinating device for the BRP and as a floor in terms of giving aid.

In Chapter 9 I employ a number of examples to further explain what I mean by the HP and the BRP, and how they would operate in the area of alien admissions. The first half of this chapter is devoted to real world phenomena. I look at U.S. alien admission practices with regard to Mexico, El Salvador, Vietnam, and so on. The second half of this chapter uses a number of hypothetical situations to fully develop these two principles. In Chapter 10 I compare alien admissions employing the HP and the BRP with present U.S. policy. Current policy is largely based on the notion of reuniting families. My point is that as admirable as this policy is, the duties under this policy are not as strong as they are under the HP and the BRP. Not only is the original separation of family members freely chosen, but any "harm" in keeping families apart would not reach the same threshold as the harm protected against under the HP and the BRP. I employ the same kind of analysis in my discussion of the past and present U.S. policy of admitting those coming from communist countries. Some individuals in these countries might meet BRP criteria; however, those who are not singled out for persecution should not be given aid or admission ahead of individuals who we have duties to under the HP and the BRP. As a final point, I explore some of the policy implications of the alien admission system proposed in these pages.

There are a few issues to address in closing. The first is to point out that, while my primary concern is to frame a theoretical basis for an alien admission system, in some instances I will also discuss other forms of "aid." One reason for this is that I see alien admissions as a form of aid, but a very special form of aid, that is dictated only under certain circumstances. Another point that needs to be underscored is that I do not discuss a right to emigrate. Frederick Whelen has suggested that a right to emigrate is an example of a natural right.[9] Michael Walzer takes a similar position: "But this right to control immigration does not include or entail the right to control emigration. . . . the right to leave one country does not entail the right to enter another (any other). Immigration and emigration are morally asymmetrical."[10] My focus is on duties that nations will have to admit certain strangers. This is not to say that the right to emigrate is not important. However, the more important question is which other nations will have a duty to admit strangers from other lands, and for what reasons.

As a final point, I wish to reiterate that I do not profess to treat all alien admission questions. In fact, I do not treat very many issues that comprise the current alien admissions debate. What I have tried to do is to frame a deeper theory of alien admissions which might serve as a useful means of answering many of the "easier" alien admission questions facing this nation today and, most assuredly, tomorrow.

NOTES

1. See generally *Fong Yue Ting v. U.S.*, 149 U.S. 698 (1893), for a good discussion of the traditional international law approach.

2. 149 U.S. at 707.
3. Charles Beitz, *Political Theory and International Relations* (Princeton: Princeton University Press, 1979).
4. See Robert Tucker, *The Inequality of Nations* (Colorado Springs: Research Committee, 1977).
5. See Stephen B. Young, "Between Sovereigns: A Re-examination of the Refugee's Status," in *Transnational Legal Problems of Refugees, 1982 Michigan Yearbook of International Legal Studies* (New York: Clark Boardman, Company, Ltd., 1982); see also Terry Nardin, *Law, Morality, and the Relations of States* (Princeton: Princeton University Press, 1983).
6. Michael Teitelbaum, "Right Versus Right: Immigration and Refugee Policy in the United States," *Foreign Affairs* 59 (1980): 21–59.
7. See Jonathon Power, *Migrant Workers in Western Europe and the United States* (Oxford: Pergamon Press, 1979).
8. S. 529, 98th Cong., 1st sess. (passed in Senate May 18, 1983); H.R. 1510, 98th Cong., 2d sess. (passed in House June 20, 1984). The conference committee was unable to reach agreement on several issues, most notably the cost of the legalization program, and this legislation eventually died. On September 19, 1985 the Senate passed this term's version of Simpson-Mazzoli, S. 1200, by a 69–30 margin.
9. Frederick Whelen, "Citizenship and the Right to Leave," *American Political Science Review* 75 (1981): 636–53.
10. Michael Walzer, "The Distribution of Membership," in Peter Brown and Henry Shue, eds., *Boundaries: National Autonomy and Its Limits* (Totowa, N.J.: Rowman and Littlefield, 1981), 10. This article can also be found in Michael Walzer, *Spheres of Justice* (New York: Basic Books, 1983).

Part I
Theories for Admitting Aliens

Chapter 1
Michael Walzer

Two themes stand out in Michael Walzer's writings that are quite relevant to the question of alien admissions. These are community and affinity. In this chapter I take up each of these concepts in turn, and ask how each would fit into a larger theory of alien admissions.

By community Walzer means that certain groups of individuals not only share a certain physical space, but they also share a common heritage, a common language, a means of governing, and so on. What Walzer means by affinity is that individuals in one society will have some identity with certain members of other societies, perhaps an entire society, based on some important shared trait. It is the tension between these two phenomena that forms the basis of a Walzerian alien admission system.

COMMUNITY

Michael Walzer is one of the most persistent proponents of the idea of political community, and also one of the staunchest defenders of the autonomy of that community.[1] Walzer sums up the essence of community this way:

4   Theories for Admitting Aliens

Here, then, is a more precise account of the social contract: it is an agreement to redistribute the resources of the members in accordance with some shared understanding of their needs, subject to ongoing political determination in detail. The contract is a moral bond. It connects the strong and the weak, the lucky and the unlucky, the rich and the poor, creating a union that transcends all differences of interest, drawing its strength from history, culture, religion, language, and so on.[2]

Because of the uniqueness of each community, Walzer is also quite adamant that nation-states should not be interfered with by outside actors. Perhaps the extremity of his position is best exemplified in his belief that military intervention, except in the most horrible circumstances, is not justifiable: "It has to be stressed that there is no right to be protected against the consequences of domestic failure, even against a bloody repression."[3]

The idea of the political community has a rich historical tradition that I will only briefly mention here. In fact, few political philosophers have not addressed this concept in one form or another. The preeminence that Walzer places on community, however, puts him in the company of writers like Plato, Aristotle, Rousseau, and to some extent Henry Sidgwick.[4]

The two great Greek thinkers, Plato and Aristotle, both viewed society as much more than a group of individuals merely living together. Instead, the state served as a moral association binding individuals into a more meaningful social unit.[5] Rousseau's ideas of the general will carry on this tradition of a moral community.[6] For Rousseau, the act of creating the political community transformed individuals from isolated entities ruled by instinct into members of a well-defined social grouping governed by justice. Moreover, the political community that was to be formed was to be a living community, one that demanded that the social and moral bonds be continually strengthened. Walzer, who shares at least some of the same views of community as Rousseau, writes:

The Rousseauian republic does not claim, then, to be an eternal shrine to the memory of its heroes; it claims something more: to be the totality of their present existence. Its collapse does not merely deprive them of glory, nor of bodily security, nor even of life itself; it is literally a fate worse than death, a fate undreamt of in Hobbes's philosophy. "If the citizen is alone," writes Rousseau, "he is nothing; if he has no more country, he has no existence; and if he is not dead, he is worse than dead."[7]

Henry Sidgwick describes community in these terms:

I think, therefore, that what is really essential to the modern conception of a State which is also a Nation is merely that the persons composing it should have, generally speaking, a consciousness of belonging to one another, of being members of one body, over and above what they derive from the mere fact of being under one government; so that if their government were destroyed by war or revolution, they would still tend to hold firmly together.[8]

As Walzer points out, although Sidgwick views a system of open borders and a world of neighborhoods as an "ideal of the future," he ultimately rejects that notion for the present.[9] Sidgwick argues that the free movement of people would throw neighbors and strangers together, and that it might interfere with efforts to raise the standard of living for the poorer classes of a particular country. In addition, the promotion of moral and intellectual culture and the efficient working of government institutions might be defeated by the continual creation of heterogeneous populations.

Walzer's views on community are premised on two related thoughts. The first is a recognition that the world is in fact divided into a number of relatively insulated communities, and these communities are important to people living in them. The second basis for Walzer's view on community is that he believes that there needs to be a limit to moral demands. His point is that when there is a duty to care for everyone, the ultimate result will be to care for no one. How far should duties carry? In a sense the descriptive serves the prescriptive. Walzer's answer is that duties essentially end at a nation's border, thus the sharp distinction he draws between "members" and "strangers." Members are citizens; all others are to be considered strangers.

Walzer's view on the role to be played by communities changes depending on the context. In *Obligations*, Walzer's focus is the individual and his argument is that the individual has certain rights vis-à-vis the political community. Walzer argues that individuals are not bound by the terms of a hypothetical social contract, particularly if that means laying one's life on the line for that community. Instead, he argues, the contract must be "lived" or "acted out" before the individual incurs obligations to the society. Walzer writes: "The myths of common citizenship and common obligation are very important to the modern state, and perhaps even generally useful to its inhabitants, but they are myths nonetheless and cannot be allowed to determine the actual commitments of actual men and women."[10]

Walzer also recognizes that a number of people living within the physical space of a community will not become obligated to that community, and he aptly titles these people "aliens." Walzer uses community in at least two different ways. One sees community as a sharing and caring among individuals living together in a common space. Under this view outsiders can, and should, be excluded. In the other view of community Walzer focuses on individual rights. Here community is seen as an intrusive force.

AFFINITY

There might be yet another way that Walzer views community. This view uses the distinction between members and strangers, but obligations do not stop at national borders. Walzer argues that individuals in one society will have certain affinities with individuals in other societies, and these affinities should serve as the basis for making certain "strangers" members. Walzer speaks of three types of affinity: ethnic, family, and ideological. In its clearest use, ethnic affinity entails an identification by nationals of a country with other nationals of that same country, wherever they are placed. Walzer uses this example: "Greeks driven from Turkey, Turks from Greece, after the wars and revolutions of the early twentieth century, had to be taken in by the states that bore their collective names, what else are such states for?"[11]

At what point do individuals lose their ethnic ties? Walzer seems to suggest that such ties are immutable. It should be pointed out that this kind of reasoning led to the internment of Japanese during World War II. At some point strangers not only become members, but their affinity with their old country will diminish. In the case of the second generation and beyond it might disappear altogether.

That there is an affinity between Americans seems indisputable: witness the Olympic Games, the America's Cup competition, or the concern for the safety of Americans abroad at the time of international strife. As we will see shortly, however, this notion of affinity seems curiously ill placed in the area of an American alien admission policy.

Another type of affinity that Walzer speaks of is an affinity between family members. The affinity itself needs no explanation or justification, but the fact that this nation relies so heavily on this principle to admit strangers does. Walzer defends the U.S. policy this way:

It is a way of acknowledging that labor mobility has a social price. Since laborers are men and women with families, one cannot admit them for the sake of their labor without accepting some commitment to their aged parents, say, or their sickly brothers and sisters.[12]

We will return to the idea of an affinity between family members at two places. Later in this chapter I will look at some empirical evidence and compare some data on alien admissions with Walzer's rationales for why family reunification is a morally justified policy. In Part II I will compare the moral justification for reuniting families through an alien admission system with other justifications for admission, particularly the two that I propose—the Harm Principle and the Basic Rights Principle.

The other type of affinity that Walzer discusses is an ideological link between individuals. Recent foreign policy aims of the United States, and much of its alien admission practices, have been premised on the idea that there is a connection between this country and all of those who seek freedom from communist oppression. As a result, the United States has admitted very large numbers of Cubans[13] and Vietnamese.[14] It has also admitted large numbers of Soviet citizens[15] (mainly Jews), Hungarian freedom fighters,[16] Polish nationals,[17] and Pakistani and Afghan rebels.[18] Apparently "ideological affinity" has strong East-West overtones. Walzer recognizes this practice, but he is also uncomfortable with its implications: "Perhaps every victim of authoritarianism and bigotry is the moral comrade of a liberal citizen; that is the argument that I would like to make. But that would press affinity too hard, and it is in any case probably unnecessary."[19]

A WALZERIAN ALIEN ADMISSION SYSTEM

For Walzer, the essence of an alien admission policy is that through this policy a community defines what it is:

But the right to choose an admissions policy ... is not merely a matter of acting in the world, exercising sovereignty, and pursuing national interests. What is at stake here is the shape of the community that acts in the world, exercises sovereignty, and so on. Admission and exclusion are at the core of communal independence.[20]

In this section I attempt to frame a Walzerian alien admission system. I begin by looking at Walzer's discussion of the relationship between the larger community and its subcommunities. After that, Walzer's notions of community and affinity are applied.

Walzer has coined a phrase that is getting a lot of play in the immigration debates: "Neighborhoods can be open only if countries are closed, or rather, only if countries are potentially closed."[21] Walzer recognizes that "larger" political communities will be comprised of a number of smaller political communities. Moreover, although the larger political community itself might not feel the disruption or the threat of arriving strangers, smaller communities might. Walzer argues that there is a self correcting mechanism at work that protects the autonomy of the smaller political community. If the larger national entity does not exclude aliens, then lower units of governments, or else neighborhoods themselves, will be forced to act as little states.

There are several points in Walzer's logic that need to be given closer scrutiny. For one thing, Walzer seems to assume that neighborhoods cannot maintain themselves as open communities. In many respects I think this is correct. However, his example of New York City at the turn of the century seems to be curious support for this proposition.[22] Walzer's statement also implicitly assumes that all neighborhoods will have the same motives. John Higham has neatly displayed how various parts of this country have had totally divergent views on the need for immigration at different points in U. S. history.[23] Linked to this, Walzer also seems to assume that the motive that is shared is always to exclude. Again, Higham has shown that this is far from universal.[24] Focusing on present day phenomena, despite the empirical evidence that strongly suggests a desire to exclude, the lackluster control of our national borders shows that the desired norm is not closed borders, at least not in many parts of the country.[25]

One of the most interesting and noteworthy social phenomena of recent years is the growing number of churches in this country that are providing Sanctuary for Salvadorans and Guatemalans who have left their respective countries, and who are now living illegally in the United States.[26] The basis for such aid is the belief that these individuals are legitimate political refugees who are being denied that status by the American government for political reasons. Sanctuary is an indication that Americans, or more precisely, some Americans, feel a special duty to aid these people because of our military involvement in that area.[27]

What is interesting to note about Sanctuary, for present purposes, is that this push to close the national borders by smaller communities is not universal. To the contrary, because the national government is unwilling to keep the door open wide enough, smaller groups of individuals are having to open up *their* neighborhoods. Sanctuary also seems to be a very good indication that ideological affinity may be a much more diffuse, and much less agreed upon, phenomenon that Walzer seems to realize.

Walzer's views of community and affinity clash, and they clash in such a way that accommodation of the two principles might not be possible. Start with Walzer's view of community: members share in each other's lives, and only members share the unique history, culture, language, mores, process of governing, and so on, of that society. All strangers, by definition, will not be imbued with these particular traits. The admission of strangers, perhaps any one stranger, would seem to cause a severe disruption to a community, at least in terms of how Walzer characterizes a community. That is, Walzer stresses the notion of a community to such an extent that alien admissions seems quite out of place.[28] Many could point to the energizing effect that newcomers have had in a country like the United States. I am quite sure that Walzer would recognize this, but the sharp theoretical distinction that he draws between members and strangers would logically seem to exclude the latter from membership at any time.[29]

A second reason for restricting the admission of aliens, perhaps even a total restriction under Walzer's view of community, is that the admission of aliens might well serve as an infringement on the autonomy of the sending states. The Communist bloc countries apparently see emigration as an infringement on their autonomy.[30] In addition, some Western political theorists also portray similar kinds of phenomena in the same light.[31] In fact, the "brain drain" phenomenon is often viewed as an infringement on the autonomy of sending societies.[32]

For many theorists, any such infringement on the autonomy of the community would give way to a respect for the autonomy of the individual. Walzer himself has argued that states cannot prevent their members from getting up and leaving.[33] However, it is not clear that Walzer's theory could make this claim, and this is where Walzer's theory seems to lead to incongruous results.[34] To begin with, if a nation sees migration as an infringement on its autonomy, then the individual's rights seem to get trumped. To understand this argument it is necessary to look at Walzer's views on the intervention of outside states when there are human rights violations in a particular country. Walzer's view is that states need to evolve in their own way. Absent a large gap in fit between community and humanity, other nations should not intervene. This is not to say that Walzer ignores human rights; he does not. However, he is willing to pay some price in protecting the autonomy of other societies and that price is some human rights violations.

If individuals possess no right to be protected by other states or international bodies against their own bloody regimes, then why, under Walzer's view, should individuals have the right to leave a regime, bloody or otherwise, when such a departure would also serve as an infringement on the autonomy of that other society? Walzer might argue that military intervention is more of an infringement on another nation's autonomy than giving refuge to foreign nationals. I would agree with this sentiment; however, what seems important under Walzer's theory is not what Western liberal philosophers think is infringement, nor even what those persecuted happen to think is infringement.[35] Instead, under Walzer's view the concern that should generally control is what other nations themselves perceive as infringement.

If the existence of communities serves to limit the obligations that individuals have, Walzer's notion of affinities has just the opposite effect (although I shall argue that Walzer does not sufficiently distinguish between affinities and obligations). Under his notion of affinities not only are there ties across national borders, but Walzer justifies admitting a whole host of strangers to membership status on the basis of certain affinities, or purported affinities.

I begin with ethnic affinities. To reiterate, ethnic affinities, in their purest form, are ties between a nation and nationals of that same nation who reside elsewhere. Thus the Greek affinity with Greeks living in Turkey, and presumably a tie between Americans at home with Americans living abroad. This situation, however, does not speak to an alien admission policy. An extended notion of ethnic affinity is based on the idea that individuals of a certain ethnic background seek to have others of that same background admitted as members to the new country.

Walzer's ideas on the restrictive national quotas legislation of the 1920s are instructive. Walzer argues that the goals of the restrictive legislation of the 1920s were impossible to achieve because we didn't have that type of society (white Anglo-Saxon) in the first place.[36] By debating the empirical Walzer misses the true significance of this legislation. What was important was not whether this country was in fact white and Anglo-Saxon, but that those in power were generally of this background and *they* possessed a strong affinity to those of the same ethnic background. Moreover, this was done at the expense of the affinities of individuals who were an ethnic minority. My reading of the 1965 Immigration Act, which abandoned the national origins quota system, was that the dominance of the majority's affinity was to end because this was unfair and had deeply racist implications. Ethnic ties still play a role in the immigration context, but they are not dispositive of any kind of affinity; in the same way, the very low number of aliens being admitted to this country from Africa should not be taken as evidence that there is little affinity between any sectors of American society and people from that continent.[37] My point is that the notion of ethnic affinities seems quite out of place in terms of present-day U.S. immigration policy. It is a system that has been tried, and instead of honoring the plurality of affinities that existed in this country it only honored the affinities of the most powerful.[38]

A less controversial form of affinity would be that between members of the same family. A different question is whether such affinities should serve as the central focus of a country's alien admission policy. There are several noteworthy aspects of Walzer's argument on family reunification in the United States. To begin with, Walzer's depiction of why we admit those we admit, as well as his empirical description of relatives that follow, are both quite misleading. Walzer's statement that "since laborers are men and women with families, one cannot admit them for the sake of their labor" suggests that we do in fact admit large numbers of individuals for the sake of their labor. This is really not true. Since 1965 the occupational preferences have only comprised 20 percent of our immigration preference quota,[39] and even this figure is misleading because workers who are admitted under these quotas also are allowed to bring their families in, and all are charged against that quota.[40]

Even more misleading, however, is Walzer's comment about accepting a commitment to the "aged parents" or "sickly brothers and sisters" of those who are currently members. In fact, Immigration and Naturalization Service (INS) data consistently show that individuals being admitted under normal flow immigration channels are generally anything but "sickly." For example, in 1979 over 30 percent of the aliens who were admitted to this country, and who declared an occupation, were white collar workers.[41] This compares with 14 percent of the American work force that falls into that category.[42] In addition, if immigrants to the United States are compared to the rest of society in the sending country, it becomes quite evident that those who migrate here are very atypical of that other society.[43]

Perhaps the final irony lies in the fact that it is questionable how much "family" there is in family reunification. The rationale behind this principle is that it is a humanitarian advance over older preference systems because although we would be sacrificing something in the way of manpower gains (yet see discussion above), still, American citizens (and some resident aliens) would now be reunited in this country with loved ones. The empirical evidence, however, suggests that love and affection are in shorter supply than the desire by immigrants for economic gain.[44] Finally, Walzer is never clear why a "commitment" to family members necessarily needs to involve admitting these individuals to this country.

In addition to these shortcomings in Walzer's writings on ethnic and family affinity, I also see some deficiencies in his view of ideological affinity. Perhaps the most serious charge against it is that it does not exist to the extent and in the form that Walzer claims. To use Walzer's example, I am not convinced that this country has ever had an ideological affinity with the Vietnamese, nor to other groups that are supposedly our ideological allies.[45] Despite the heavy military buildup in Vietnam (or perhaps because of it), and the repeated claims of a bloodbath should the North win (mostly sounded during the military buildup, and not when defeat seemed imminent), the American people have not been particularly pleased to have Vietnamese admitted to these shores.[46] Although this might not seem to be conclusive evidence against an ideological affinity, it would at least throw some doubt on Walzer's proposition.

Another shortcoming in Walzer's view of ideological affinity is that it seems to know no bounds. I think he begins on the right track. Walzer writes: "The victims of political and religious persecution, then, make the most forceful claim for admission. 'If you don't take me in,' they say, 'I shall be killed, persecuted, brutally oppressed by the rulers of my own country.' What can we reply?"[47] Walzer initially recognizes that of all those thirteen million or so refugees in the world we might have a stronger duty to some than to others.

> Toward some refugees, we may well have obligations of the same sort that we have toward fellow nationals. This is obviously the case with regard to any group whom we have helped turn into refugees. The injury we have done them makes for an affinity between us; thus Vietnamese refugees had, in a moral sense, been effectively Americanized even before they arrived on these shores.[48]

I agree with Walzer that those we have harmed will comprise a separate class from those we have not harmed; however, I believe that Walzer is mistaken when he states that "the injury we have done makes for an affinity." An affinity might arise (although it has not in this instance), but the injury we have caused does more than create an affinity. It creates an obligation to aid those we have harmed.

Although Walzer begins by discussing an affinity to those we have harmed, he then begins to broaden his scope: "But we can also be bound to help men and women persecuted or oppressed by someone else—if they are persecuted or oppressed because they are *like us*."[49] Finally, in language already partially quoted, Walzer begins to address the question of how far this duty to ideological allies should go.

> Perhaps every victim of authoritarianism and bigotry is the moral comrade of a liberal citizen; that is an argument I would like to make. But that would press affinity too hard, and it is in any case probably unnecessary. So long as the number of victims is small, the mutual-aid principle will generate similar practical results, and when the number increases, and we are forced to choose among the victims, we shall look, rightfully, for some more direct connection with our own way of life.[50]

At this point it is necessary to see just how far Walzer's theory has gone. Remember, Walzer begins with the idea that closed communities should be the norm, and that members should care for other members, and not those in other communities. However, when Walzer begins to address the question of alien admissions his ideas seem to go in the opposite direction from where they had gone previously. Walzer defends the principle of family reunification; he defends admitting to membership those illegal aliens who have worked in this country;[51] he advocates admitting those we have helped to turn into refugees. Finally, Walzer seems to suggest that we might want to admit all of those who live under unjust regimes. It is only at this point that Walzer seems to be cognizant of the fact that some limits might have to be made in terms of admissions. It is uncertain, however, how far Walzer is willing to push affinity, and what order of admission he would suggest.

The final point concerning Walzer's notion of ideological affinity is that it assumes too much common ground. That is to say, Walzer seems to assume that all citizens of a liberal state will share the same views of who is an "ideological ally," or who is "like us." Ironically enough, Walzer's views of an ideological affinity differ sharply from the views of the U.S. government. While Walzer has an affinity to "every victim of authoritarianism and bigotry," this view is not shared by the present administration which draws a sharp distinction between authoritarian and totalitarian regimes,[52] nor is it reflected in the refugee/asylum practices of the United States.[53]

In fact, it is the multiplicity of ideological affinities in a pluralist society like ours that makes this concept of "affinity" such an unworkable concept. To show this, look at the present tragedy in Africa. Jews in Israel have felt an ideological affinity to the Falasha, or black Jews. As a result, they have admitted many thousands who would otherwise have starved. Perhaps American Jews would feel the same kind of affinity and seek to admit some of this number. However, what about affinities that black Americans might feel to starving black Africans more generally? Should we honor any and all affinities that American citizens might have? If all members of a nation have to agree on an affinity (and that admission is warranted) few individuals would be admitted on the basis of an ideological affinity. If all affinities have to be honored, then we would find ourselves admitting very large numbers of foreigners. I would suggest that our refugee admissions have reflected the ideological affinities that are the strongest politically or the most vocal; however, I am not convinced that this is how our alien admission policy should work. I conclude, then, that the notion of ideological affinity is not such a workable or viable standard for alien admission practices, at least not in a nation as diverse as the United States.

CONCLUSION

Although Walzer's views and those I propose in Part II do not differ dramatically, important differences do exist and they need to be discussed. Members *can* be differentiated from nonmembers and they *should* be distinguished.[54] Communities are in fact vital to individuals, although I think Walzer greatly overstates the distinguishing features of societies. Finally, I do share Walzer's view that open-ended duties are ultimately no duties at all.

What is puzzling about Walzer's notion of affinities, then, is how open-ended they are and the far-ranging activities that they prompt. Walzer talks about ethnic, family, and ideological ties, and along with employment in the United States, all seem to warrant admission to this country. This is a much different situation from Walzer's original notion of insulated communities, and a far cry from the sharp distinction between members and strangers. This is not to say that I totally disagree with Walzer in terms of admission practices; I do not. Nations are obligated to admit certain strangers. I think some of the rationales for admission that Walzer presents are compelling, but others are not. Part II is devoted to determining such issues.

NOTES

1. I think this in general is true, although as I mention later, one of the difficulties in interpreting Walzer is that he occasionally changes his focus from the community at large to the individual, and in doing so he seems to change the entire nature of his theory.

2. Michael Walzer, *Spheres of Justice* (New York: Basic Books, 1983), 82.

3. Michael Walzer, *Just and Unjust Wars* (New York: Basic Books, 1977), 88.

4. See generally Carl Friedrich, "The Concept of Community in the

History of Political and Legal Philosophy," *Nomos II* (Community) (New York: Liberal Arts Press, 1959).

5. For a general discussion see J. W. Gough, *The Social Contract*, 2d ed. (Oxford: Clarendon Press, 1957).

6. See Ernest Baker, *Social Contracts: Essays By Locke, Hume, and Rousseau* (New York: Oxford University Press, 1962).

7. Michael Walzer, *Obligations: Essays on Civil Disobedience, War, and Citizenship* (Cambridge: Harvard University Press, 1970), 93.

8. Henry Sidgwick, *The Elements of Politics* (London: Macmillan and Company, 1919), 224.

9. Michael Walzer, "The Distribution of Membership," in Peter Brown and Henry Shue, eds., *Boundaries: National Autonomy and Its Limits* (Totowa, N.J.: Rowman and Littlefield, 1981), 7.

10. Walzer, *Obligations*, 118.

11. Walzer, "The Distribution of Membership," 12.

12. Ibid.

13. Report to the Congress, *Refugee Resettlement Program*, Department of Health and Human Services, Office of Refugee Resettlement, (Washington, D.C.: GPO, 1983). Since 1959 over 800,000 Cubans have been admitted to the United States as "refugees." It should also be noted that this number does not include the 125,000 Cuban "entrants" who were lawfully admitted in 1980.

14. Ibid. Up to FY 1982 over 620,000 Vietnamese refugees had been admitted to the United States.

15. Ibid. Between 1975 and 1979 more than 100,000 Russian refugees came to the United States.

16. In the 1950s the United States admitted approximately 38,000 refugees of Hungarian descent. See S. Rep. No. 256, 96th Cong., 1st sess. 6, reprinted in *1980 U.S. Code Cong. and Admin. News*, 141, 146 (Table 1—Historical Summary of Refugee Parole Action).

17. *Refugee Resettlement* (1983). In FY 81 the United States admitted 2,000 Poles, and in FY 82 an additional 6,600.

18. *Refugee Resettlement* (1985). The United States has admitted over 13,000 Afghan and Pakistani rebels since 1980.

19. Walzer, "The Distribution of Membership," 21.

20. Ibid., 32.

21. Ibid., 9.

22. Ibid.

23. John Higham, *Strangers in the Land* (New York: Atheneum Press, 1960).

24. George Grassmuck has similarly shown how various regional differences, and demographic characteristics, explain a large part of the

differences in legislative voting on immigration legislation in the 1920s. George Grassmuck (unpublished paper, copy with author).

25. For a very insightful presentation of the motivations at play here see Michael Piore, *Birds of Passage: Migrant Labor and Industrial Society* (New York: Cambridge University Press, 1980).

26. See George Volsky, "U.S. Churches Offer Sanctuary to Aliens Facing Deportation," *New York Times*, Apr. 8, 1983; Stuart Taylor Jr., "More Churches Join in Offering Sanctuary," *New York Times*, Sept. 21, 1983.

27. See "Sanctuary Worker Convicted in Alien Trial," *New York Times*, May 15, 1984, ("Miss Merkt testified that she did not consider what she had done to be against the law since she considered the Salvadorans political refugees."), p.7. See also Mark Gibney, "Seeking Sanctuary: A Special Duty for the U.S.?" *Commonweal*, May 18, 1984, 295.

28. Walzer writes: "Communal life and liberty requires the existence of 'relatively self-enclosed arenas of political development.' Break into the enclosures and you destroy the communities.... Against foreigners, individuals have a right to a state of their own." "The Moral Standing of States: A Response to Four Critics," *Philosophy and Public Affairs* 9 (1980), 228. Although Walzer was speaking of military intervention, I think the analogy would logically extend to alien admissions because of the extremity of his members-strangers distinction.

29. David Martin seems to think that relatively high levels of immigration are possible under Walzer's theory. See "Due Process and the Treatment of Aliens," *University of Pittsburgh Law Review* 44 (1983): 199.

30. One of the ironies in the U.S. policy of helping Haiti prevent the exodus of "boat people" because such emigration was considered illegal by the Haitian authorities, was the fact that at the same time the United States was castigating the Soviet Union for restricting what the Soviets considered "illegal migration." For a defense of U.S. interdiction policy see U.S. Cong., Senate, Hearings before the Subcommittee on Immigration and Refugee Policy of the Committee on the Judiciary, *United States as a Country of Mass First Asylum*, 97th Cong., 1st sess. July 31, 1981, (prepared statement of Thomas Enders, Assistant Secretary of State for Inter-American Affairs), 3.

31. David Baldwin posits the idea of foreign aid as intervention in "Foreign Aid, Intervention, and Influence," *World Politics* 21 (1969): 425–37.

32. See *The Reverse Transfer of Technology: A Survey of Its Main Features, Causes, and Policy Implications*, United Nations Conference on Trade and Development (New York: United Nations, 1979).

33. Walzer, "The Distribution of Membership," 10.

34. One of Walzer's four critics writes, "Why should Walzer's individual right to national autonomy be more basic than other human rights, such as freedom from terror, torture, material deprivation, illiteracy, and suppressed speech." Gerald Doppelt, "Statism Without Foundations," *Philosophy and Public Affairs* 9 (1975): 403.

35. In "The Moral Standing of States" Walzer continually stresses the idea that citizens of societies we may think are unjust or illegitimate will fight against foreigners who are attempting to intervene militarily in that country. Walzer uses this as proof that determinations by foreigners about the legitimacy of other regimes may not reflect the true state of affairs. What Walzer does not spend enough time on is the question of how many citizens actually have to fight to show that at least as far as other nations are concerned this particular nation is legitimate. Walzer writes: "For as long as substantial numbers of citizens believe themselves bound and are prepared, for whatever reasons, to fight, an attack upon their state would constitute aggression." ("The Moral Standing of States," 213). Walzer overlooks the fact that unjust practices might be practiced only on certain sectors of the populace, thus there might not be any motivational problems is getting those not affected to fight. Walzer is also unclear in terms of what he means by "substantial numbers." What if a large percentage of the population (those singled out for persecution, for example) fervently desired military intervention, but there were still "substantial numbers" who would fight?

36. Walzer, "The Distribution of Membership," 11.

37. For example, in 1979 out of worldwide total of 460,348 aliens who were admitted to the United States, only 5,198 were from Africa, U.S. Dept. of Justice, *Statistical Yearbook of the Immigration and Naturalization Service, 1979*. The number of refugees admitted from Africa has also been quite minimal, averaging around 3,000 the past few years, Report to the Congress, *Refugee Resettlement Program*, Department of Health and Human Services, Office of Refugee Resettlement, (Washington, D.C.: GPO, 1984).

38. Other nations have had different kinds of problems in defining "affinity." The rather hostile reception in England accorded black members of the British Commonwealth seems to call into question whether such an affinity exists. See Daniel Lawrence, *Black Migrants: White Natives; A Study of Race Relations in Nottingham* (Cambridge: Cambridge University Press, 1974); Sheila Patterson, *Immigration and Race Relations in Britain 1960–1967* (Oxford: Oxford University Press, 1969); David Dixon, "Thatcher's People: The British Nationality Act of 1981," *Journal of Law and Society* 10 (1983): 161–80.

20   Theories for Admitting Aliens

39. See § 203, 8 U.S. C. 1153 of the *Immigration and Nationality Act (INA)* as Amended to September 1, 1980.

40. Ibid. Approximately 94 percent of normal flow alien admissions is based on family relations. See the *Statistical Yearbook of the Immigration and Naturalization Service, 1979*, Table 7a, p. 16.

41. Ibid., Table 8, p. 18.

42. See International Labour Office, *1979 Yearbook of Labour Statistics* (Geneva: International Labour Office, 1979); see also Charles Keely, "Effects of U.S. Immigration Law on Manpower Characteristics," *Demography* 12 (1975): 179–91.

43. For example, in 1979 57 percent of those migrating to the United States from Iran under normal flow immigration channels, and who stated an occupation, were either professional, technical and kindred workers, or managers and administrators. Only 6 percent of the Iranian population falls into these high socioeconomic categories. For that same year, 68 percent of those migrating from India were in this occupational category compared with only 3.7 percent of the population of India. Forty-two percent of those coming from Thailand in 1979 were of this "white collar" occupational background compared with only 3 percent of the general population. The list goes on and on. The comparisons were made by obtaining occupational backgrounds by country in the International Labour Office yearbook, and then comparing these numbers with the occupational breakdowns in the Immigration and Naturalization Service yearbook.

44. See Marta Tienda, "Familism and Structural Assimilation of Mexican Immigrants," *International Migration Review* 14 (1980) 383–408; see also Rosemary Stevens, Louis Wolf Goodman, and Stephen S. Mick, *The Alien Doctors* (New York: Wiley Pub., 1978); Animesh Ghoshal, "Political Versus Economic Refugees," *U.S. Immigration Policy and the National Interest, Staff Report of the Select Commission on Immigration and Refugee Policy*, appendix C ("The general consensus is that migration tends to follow economic opportunity, though education, urbanization, and other factors are also significant."), 214.

45. For example, John Scanlan describes how it was necessary for President Eisenhower to hire a private public relations firm in order to "sell" the Hungarians being admitted to this country as freedom fighters in the 1950s. See John Scanlan, "Immigration Law and the Illusion of Numerical Control," *U. Miami Law Review* 36 (1982): 849. Cuban refugees do not seem particularly popular with U.S. citizens either. For example, in 1980 a Gallup poll was taken with regard to the "Freedom Flotillas" at that time. When asked, "Do you feel the Cuban emigration is good for the United States because it shows widespread dissatisfac-

tion with Castro's government, or do you feel it is bad for the United States because it is difficult and expensive to take in so many refugees?," the responses were: Good—19 percent, Bad—59 percent, Both—13 percent, and Don't Know—9 percent. When asked, "So far 40,000 Cuban refugees have come into the United States and 200,000 more may wish to come. How many more, if any, should the United States accept?," the responses were: All or Most—13 percent, Some—12 percent, None—40 percent, Only those with Relatives in the U.S.—28 percent, and Don't Know—7 percent. See David M. Alpern et al., "Carter and the Cuban Influx," *Newsweek*, May 26, 1980, 22–28.

46. In a 1975 Gallup poll, when asked whether evacuated South Vietnamese refugees should be permitted to live in the United States or not, 36 percent said yes, 52 percent said no, and 12 percent expressed no opinion. *Gallup Opinion Index* (Princeton: American Institute of Public Opinion, May 1975), 2. In 1979 another Gallup poll asked this question about Indochinese "boat people": "Would you favor or oppose the U.S. relaxing its immigration policies so that many of these people could come to live in the United States?," the responses were 32 percent in favor, 57 percent opposed, and 11 percent had no opinion. When further asked, "If some of these people came to live in this community do you think they would be welcomed or not?," the responses were surprising: 57 percent said the refugees would be welcome, 30 percent said they would not be, and 13 percent had no opinion. Finally, when asked "Would you, yourself, like to see some of these people come to live in this community, or not?," the responses were 47 percent in favor, 40 percent would not want the refugees in that community, and 13 percent expressed no opinion. Although individuals seemed more confident of their own altruism than what they thought the nation, as a whole, would display, it seems difficult to look at this data and conclude that this is an indication of an ideological affinity. *Gallup Opinion Index* (Princeton: American Institute of Public Opinion, September 1979), 8–11.

47. Walzer, "The Distribution of Membership," p. 12. Alex Aleinikoff has suggested a similar rationale. "What distinguishes the alien applying for asylum—if the claim is valid—from all other applicants for entry is precisely the lack of a political community to return to.... Does not this fact, the lack of a political community of which the asylees can be a part in their home countries, strengthen their request for admission here?" T. Alexander Aleinikoff, "Aliens, Due Process and Community Ties: A Response to Martin," *University of Pittsburgh Law Review* 44 (1983): 257.

48. Walzer, "The Distribution of Membership," 20.

49. Ibid.
50. Ibid., 21.
51. Ibid., 26–32.
52. For the clearest description of this distinction see Jeanne Kirkpatrick, "Dictatorships and Double Standards," in Howard J. Wiarda, ed., *Human Rights and U.S. Human Rights Policy* (Washington, D.C.: American Enterprise Institute, 1982).
53. See Michael Posner and Susan Kaplan, "Who Should We Let In?" *Human Rights* (Summer, 1981); see also Arthur C. Helton, "Political Asylum Under the 1980 Refugee Act: An Unfulfilled Promise," *University of Michigan Journal of Law Reform* 17 (1984): 243–64.
54. Alex Aleinikoff does not think the distinction between members and strangers holds in this society: "The idea of a political community sharing similar ideas of the meaning of membership and the scope of the common enterprise does not aptly describe a nation as diverse, as pluralistic as the United States. To say that there are serious political and social differences among groups of Americans is to state the obvious. No one ideology, religion or culture unites us. Ethnic and racial lines continue to separate Americans into distinct, self-identifying groups." Aleinikoff, "Community Ties," 240–41. I would position myself somewhere between those who would see some kind of homogeneous political community in this country, and those who see very little sense of community.

Chapter 2
John Rawls

John Rawls, like Michael Walzer, works within a framework of the traditional nation-state.[1] Rawls offers his two principles as a prototype for an ideal society.[2] "I shall be satisfied if it is possible to formulate a reasonable conception of justice for the basic structure of society conceived for the time being as a closed system isolated from other societies."[3] Rawls's focus, then, is almost solely domestic. At one point Rawls states that he will extend his two principles of justice worldwide;[4] but as Brian Barry has quite effectively shown, the result is not what one would have expected.[5] Instead of a worldwide distribution of social goods, Rawls argues that what would emerge from an international original position would be agreement on the idea that governments are autonomous enterprises, and that citizens of a country have the right to settle their own affairs without the intervention of foreign powers. Another principle Rawls believes would be accepted is that treaties should be kept. In short, Rawls's position on international relations evinces the rather traditional view of the nation-state noted at the outset of this work.

Here I attempt to extend Rawls's theory. I begin by noting several phenomena that Rawls discusses that might cause him to address questions of alien admissions. Although he does not take this tack, there are elements of his theory that quite naturally lend themselves to a discussion of such issues. What emerges is a "Rawlsian" alien admission policy that is based upon the idea of autonomous individuals, and the need to protect and preserve their autonomy. The second part of this chapter analyzes the Brian Barry-Charles Beitz critique of Rawls's theory.

A RAWLSIAN ALIEN ADMISSION SYSTEM

Rationales for Admission

The notion of a shared community plays a central role in John Rawls's theory:

> The public knowledge that we are living in a society in which we can depend upon others to come to our assistance in difficult circumstances is itself of great value.... The primary value of the principle is not measured by the help we actually receive but rather by the sense of confidence and trust in other men's good intentions and the knowledge that they are there if we need them.[6]

Like Michael Walzer's theory, Rawls's theory generally draws a distinction between members and strangers (although he does not use this terminology). Members share in a common life with other members, but not with strangers. The parallel between the two philosophers is extended further because Rawls is also willing to loosen this distinction. The assistance that individuals sharing in a community give one another is based on what Rawls describes as a natural duty to aid. The first time Rawls mentions such a duty he speaks of it in broad terms:

> Whereas all obligations are accounted for by the principle of fairness, there are many natural duties, positive and negative.... The following are examples of natural duties: the duty of helping another when he is in need or jeopardy, provided that one can do so without excessive risk or loss to oneself; the duty not to harm or injure another; and the duty not to cause unnecessary suffering.[7]

Rawls continues:

Now in contrast with obligations, it is characteristic of natural duties that they apply to us without regard to our voluntary acts. Moreover, they have no necessary connection with institutions or social practices; their content is not, in general, defined by the rules of these arrangements.... A further feature of natural duties is that they hold between persons irrespective of their institutional relationships; they obtain between all as equal moral persons. In this sense the natural duties are owed not only to definite individuals, say to those cooperating together in a particular social arrangement, but to persons generally.[8]

The balance that Rawls seeks to achieve, then, is essentially the same that Walzer sought: the need to respect and maintain the autonomy of well-ordered communities and those who live in these communities, while at the same time we seek to meet the demands of those in serious need wherever they live.

Although Rawls's ideal is a just, well-ordered society, he is also cognizant that states have not reached that end. Some states will respect the autonomy of their citizens while others will not. Rawls describes the obligations to unjust societies in these terms:

Acquiescence in, or even consent to, clearly unjust institutions does not give rise to obligations. It is generally agreed that extorted promises are void *ab initio*. But similarly, unjust social arrangements are themselves a kind of extortion, even violence, and consent to them does not bind.[9]

Not every member of a society will agree on whether a particular social arrangement or state is just or not. Rawls describes those in deep opposition to a certain regime this way:

The militant, for example, is much more deeply opposed to the existing political system [than others in that society]. He does not accept it as one which is nearly just or reasonably so; he believes either that it departs widely from its professed principles or that it pursues a mistaken conception of justice altogether.... he seeks by well-framed militant acts of disruption and resistance, and the like, to attack the prevalent view of justice or to force a movement in the desired direction.[10]

Unjust practices are not the state's preserve. Rawls also discusses the phenomenon of intolerant groups in a society, such as political parties that attempt to suppress constitutional liberties, or religious groups that seek to eliminate religious freedom for others. Rawls describes two scenarios. In the first intolerant groups are in a minority:

> The question of tolerating the intolerant is directly related to the stability of a well-ordered society regulated by the two principles.... If an intolerant sect appears in a well-ordered society, the others should keep in mind the inherent stability of their institutions. The liberties of the intolerant may persuade them to a belief in freedom.... So even if an intolerant sect should arise, provided that it is not so strong initially that it can impose its will straightway, or does not grow so rapidly that the psychological principle has no time to take hold, it will tend to lose its intolerance and accept liberty of conscience.[11]

Intolerant groups, however, might be dominant. "Of course, the intolerant sect may be so strong initially or growing so fast that the forces making for stability cannot convert it to liberty. This situation presents a practical dilemma which philosophy alone cannot resolve."[12]

In this section I have looked at certain unjust practices in a society which Rawls has discussed. Some of these practices are carried out by the state, while others are practiced by private groups in the society. I now turn to possible resolutions of these problems.

The Basis for Admission

Rawls is not very certain how the various unjust practices that he discusses would be resolved. For example, Rawls posits that when intolerant groups are a minority in a society they will eventually become tolerant as they learn to function as integral members of a well-ordered society. Rawls does not have a resolution to the problem when intolerant groups are not such a small minority.[13] He states that this "situation presents a practical dilemma which philosophy alone cannot resolve," and leaves matters like that. The problem of unjust institutions also has a partial solution. Rawls spends some time talking about the need at times to confront an unjust government through civil disobedience, but he purposely limits his discussion to "the special case of a nearly just society, one that is well-ordered for the most part but in which some serious violations of justice nevertheless do occur."[14]

Rawls sees civil disobedience as a means of last resort. "We may suppose that the normal appeals to the political majority have already been made in good faith and that they have failed. The legal means of redress have proved of no avail."[15] Although this is a general rule, there will be instances when this rule should be ignored.

> Some cases may be so extreme that there may be no duty to use first only legal means of political opposition. If, for example, the legislature were to enact some outrageous violation of equal liberty, say by forbidding the religion of a weak and defenseless minority, we surely would not expect that sect to oppose the law by normal political procedures. Indeed, even civil disobedience might be much too mild, the majority having already convicted itself of wantonly unjust and overtly hostile aims.[16]

There are two things to note about Rawls's attempts to deal with unjust practices. The first is that he does not deal with the most egregious cases. Instead, he purposely limits his discussion to nearly just societies, and he declines to comment on situations where intolerant groups are quite powerful in a society. The second point is that Rawls essentially envisions domestic resolutions, if a resolution is possible. Thus his discussion of the intolerant becoming tolerant; acts of civil disobedience against the government; and the fact that militant acts will at times be justified, although Rawls does not specify when such acts would be justified and what such acts would entail.[17]

Although Rawls does seem to limit possible resolutions of unjust practices to a single society, it is not necessary to do so. In fact, resolution might be better accomplished through intersocietal means. I have already pointed out that Rawls specifies that the natural duty to aid can extend across national boundaries. The clearest example of this occurs in his discussion of conscription and just wars:

> Now I shall assume that since conscription is a drastic interference with the basic liberties of equal citizenship, it cannot be justified by any

needs less compelling than those of national security. In a well-ordered society (or in one nearly just), these needs are determined by the end of preserving just institutions. Conscription is permissible only if it is demanded for the defense of liberty itself, including here not only the liberties of the citizens of the society in question, but also those of persons in other societies as well.[18]

It is my position that Rawls could accomplish much of what he would like to accomplish through an alien admission system. Stay with the example of just wars. Conscription serves as an interference on individual liberty. Being exposed to the dangers of war, one can presume, would serve as an even greater interference. In addition, war threatens to severely harm innocent civilians, those whose rights are sought to be protected in the first place. Instead of war to protect human rights, the basic rights of individuals in other countries might be better protected by having outside nations grant admission to those persecuted. There would be less interference with the autonomy of the soldier (if conscription would now still be needed under these circumstances), less infringement on the autonomy of societies where war would be waged,[19] and the possibility of harm to war innocents will also be greatly lessened.[20] I conclude, then, that in terms of meeting the civil liberties of individuals in other societies, Rawls's theory would benefit from a system of alien admissions. An alien admission system would also help address situations where intolerant groups are in fact a majority. Philosophers *do* have an answer: those who suffer serious persecution from such groups could receive aid through admission to other societies.

One of Rawls's main objectives in framing his theory is the protection of individual autonomy. He repeatedly contrasts his own theory with utilitarianism which, he argues, does not protect this autonomy.[21] Note from the outline provided above that the main objective of a Rawlsian alien admission system is the protection of the autonomy of individuals. What does it mean to protect the autonomy of the individual? A recent law review article[22] on U.S. immigration policy has taken the following language from *A Theory of Justice* and attempted to frame a "Rawlsian" response to immigration issues: "what is necessary is that there should be for each individual at least one community of shared interests to which he belongs and where he finds his endeavors confirmed by his associates."[23]

This reading is suspect. In language almost immediately preceding that quoted above, Rawls states: "It normally suffices that for each person there is some association (one or more) to which he belongs and within which the activities that are rational for him are publicly affirmed by others."[24] I argue that Rawls is not speaking of approbation by the larger political community, as the first quote taken out of context would suggest, but of smaller associations in that society. More importantly, social approbation would not be a compelling reason that would obligate other nations to aid, through alien admissions or otherwise. When Rawls is speaking of a natural duty to aid he is talking about helping those in serious need. When individuals in one society are drafted to fight for the civil rights of individuals in another society we can assume that the liberties to be defended are basic liberties, and that the violations are serious. Those who "need" social approbation do not present the same kind of claim as those in serious physical danger. A natural duty to aid does not arise when we are speaking of social approbation.

CRITIQUES OF RAWLS

Brian Barry and Charles Beitz have both argued that an individual's autonomy is not protected when this person does not have food or shelter.[25] Both believe that Rawls's difference principle should be extended worldwide. Barry and Beitz base their critique on two related grounds. The first is that if individuals are as risk averse as their behavior in the original position indicates, then they would seek to ensure that they did not emerge from the original position and find themselves in a poverty-ridden society. Barry's earlier comments reflect this position. A second claim that Barry and Beitz rely upon is that the worldwide distribution of natural resources is morally arbitrary. An important part of Rawls's argument is that individuals do not have any special right to those things in the world that are morally arbitrary. One example of what Rawls considers to be morally arbitrary is an individual's natural talents. Beitz responds:

30   Theories for Admitting Aliens

I conclude that the natural distribution of resources is a purer case of something being "arbitrary from a moral point of view" than the distribution of talents. Not only can one not be said to deserve the resources under one's feet; the other grounds on which one might assert an initial claim to talents are absent in the case of resources, as well.[26]

I believe that Barry and Beitz deliver a telling blow to the basis of Rawls's framework.[27] Individual autonomy is not protected when individuals do not have the means for subsistence. The lack of food and shelter is just as devastating to an individual, if not in fact more devastating, than persecution from unjust regimes or intolerant groups. The more difficult question is what other nations in the world should do to meet this need. Here analysis gets fuzzier.

Barry suggests that nations could begin by providing more aid than they do at present.[28] He then argues that nations with open space should increase their immigration quotas as a way of moving directly towards greater equality in the proceeds of exploiting natural resources. However, Barry is not optimistic that increased migration will accomplish much in terms of sharing access to natural resources. In addition, by opening up a nation's borders there will be assimilation problems as well as a threat to domestic workers. Despite these perceived shortcomings, Barry ultimately concludes that increasing immigration is by far the most immediate and direct way of making access to natural resources more equal, and that nations that turn down this option must accept the duty of providing substantial transfer payments.

One of the main purposes of my work is to present a case for the idea that alien admissions should play an integral part in meeting the basic rights of individuals in other lands. However, in the process of attempting to accomplish this we also need to ensure that we do not trample on the autonomy of the "have" nations and their members. One distinction that is vital is that between the equal use or exploitation of the world's resources on the one hand, and the equal enjoyment from the exploitation of the world's resources on the other. When Barry first talks about immigration as a means of moving directly towards greater equality in the proceeds of exploiting natural resources he is talking of the latter. However, when he talks about making access to natural resources more equal, he is adopting the former position. Both of these methods could be used in attempting to meet the subsistence needs of others, but the two methods would take vastly different approaches. The second seems to honor what Walzer describes as the autonomy of communities. This approach recognizes that even if natural resources within a community can be considered morally arbitrary, the communities themselves are not. The second approach, then, would not call for open borders, but relatively closed borders, but with a sharing of the proceeds from the exploitation of the world's resources. The first approach, which talks in terms of "equal access" to the world's resources, does not go far enough in respecting existing communities. The policy that would emerge from such a view would be open borders. This result would seriously infringe on the communal processes of resource-rich countries. Moreover, this would ultimately result in a loss of individual autonomy as well. One does not have to go as far as Rousseau to understand that communities are vital to individuals.

CONCLUSION

A Rawlsian alien admission system would seek to protect the autonomy of individuals in other lands. That is, nations could meet their natural duty to aid those in serious need who live in other countries through an alien admission system. I have argued here that such a system would be much less of an interference on individual liberty and communal autonomy than other policies, such as war.

Such a system would need to balance the concern for communal preservation with the concern for meeting the serious needs of others. This would mean relatively closed borders. Large numbers of strangers will disrupt the autonomy of a community and its members. One way of limiting alien admissions would be to restrict it to those in very serious need, and where admission, rather than other means of assistance, is vital. Even with such restrictions, it is important to note that the international application of Rawls's natural duty to aid does not single out any type of relationship between societies that might obligate one particular society to provide aid to individuals in another. Instead, there is a general duty to all of those in need. The reader is reminded of Walzer's statement that the duty to aid all will ultimately mean the duty to care for no one. In Part II I will address such matters.

Charles Beitz and Brian Barry question whether the lack of subsistence facing millions of people serves as much of an infringement on individual autonomy as those phenomena that Rawls discusses. This is a position that I agree with. What is not readily apparent is how this position translates into a viable alien admission system. I have argued here that it is quite important to distinguish between the proceeds of the exploitation of the world's natural resources, and "equal access" to these same resources. I should point out that I do not pursue this particular discussion in Part I because I am limiting my discussion to alien admission matters, although the general issue of aid is very much tied in with this topic.

NOTES

1. John Rawls, *A Theory of Justice* (Cambridge: Harvard University Press, 1971).
2. Ibid., 302. The two principles are: First Principle—Each person is to have an equal right to the most extensive total system of equal basic liberties compatible with a similar system of liberty for all. Second Principle—Social and economic inequalities are to be arranged so that they are both: (1) to the greatest benefit of the least advantaged, consistent with the just savings principle, and (2) attached to offices and positions open to all under conditions of fair equality of opportunity.
3. Ibid., 8.
4. Ibid., 378.
5. "Surely, viewing things from the 'original position' one would at all costs wish to avoid this kind of poverty if we turned out to live in a poor country even if this meant being less well off than otherwise if one turned out to live in North America or Western Europe." Brian Barry, *The Liberal Theory of Justice* (Oxford: Clarendon Press, 1973), 130.
6. Rawls, *A Theory of Justice*, 339.
7. Ibid., 114.
8. Ibid.

9. Ibid., 343. See also Hannah Pitkin, "Obligations and Consent I," *American Political Science Review* 59 (1965): 990–99.

10. Rawls, *A Theory of Justice*, 367.

11. Ibid., 219.

12. Ibid.

13. Rawls does not address what would happen if the intolerant who were a minority did not in fact become tolerant over time. We might presume, however, that persecution would not be as much of a concern here as it would when the intolerant were a majority.

14. Rawls, *A Theory of Justice*, 363.

15. Ibid., 373.

16. Ibid.

17. Ibid., 368.

18. Ibid., 380.

19. What would argue against military actions by one country in another country, even in defense of civil liberties, is that Rawls takes a position on national autonomy that is quite similar to Walzer's. As noted earlier, one of the "agreements" reached in the original position writ large is "the principle of self-determination, the right of a people to settle its own affairs without the intervention of foreign powers." (Rawls, *A Theory of Justice*, 378). This nonintervention principle would have to be balanced against protecting the rights of individuals in other societies.

20. Mark Wicclair argues that in the international social contract individuals would agree to a rule of limited intervention because of the possibility of human rights violations. Without taking a position on this matter, I would point out that if individuals agree to this, surely they would agree to a less intrusive means of protecting human rights through alien admissions. See Mark Wicclair, "Rawls and the Principle of Nonintervention," in H. Gene Blocker and Elizabeth H. Smith, eds., *John Rawls's Theory of Social Justice: An Introduction* (Athens: Ohio University Press, 1980).

21. See generally *A Theory of Justice*, chapter 6. It should be noted that the same kind of charge has been made against Rawls's theory itself. See R. M. Hare, "Rawls' Theory of Justice," in Norm Daniels, ed. *Reading Rawls* (New York: Basic Books, 1975).

22. Note, "Immigration Policy and the Rights of Aliens," *Harvard Law Review* 96 (1983): 1324, n.61.

23. Rawls, *A Theory of Justice*, 442.

24. Ibid., 441.

25. Charles Beitz, *Political Theory and International Relations* (Princeton: Princeton University Press, 1979); see also Charles Beitz, "Bounded

Morality: Justice and the State in World Politics," *International Organization* 33 (1979): 405–24; Brian Barry, *Rich Countries and Poor Countries* (unpublished manuscript, quoted with permission of author). Other theorists who seem to come to the same conclusions as Beitz and Barry, but through different means, are: Peter Brown, "Food as National Property," in Peter Brown and Henry Shue, eds., *Food Policy: The Responsibility of the United States in the Life and Death Choices* (New York: Free Press, 1977); Hillel Steiner, "The Natural Right to the Means of Production," *Philosophical Quarterly* 27 (1977): 41–49; Tim Scanlon, "Rawls' Theory of Justice," in Norm Daniels, ed., *Reading Rawls* (New York: Basic Books, 1975).

26. Beitz, *Political Theory*, 140.

27. Beitz limits his discussion to foreign assistance, with such aid going to the world's "worst-off" group. I will address this type of response in Part II when I address T. D. Campbell's position.

28. Barry, *Rich Countries and Poor Countries*, see generally chapter 7.

Chapter 3
Peter Singer and Henry Shue

We began Part I by looking at the ideas of Michael Walzer. We noted Walzer's position that members should concern themselves with aiding other members of a particular society, Walzer's point being that given the responsibility for all, the natural reaction will be to care for no one. We have also noted a number of exceptions that Walzer seems to make to his rule, but his general proposition is still that a nation should care for its own. Rawls was the next theorist whom we looked at. Like Walzer's, Rawls's position seems to be that well-ordered societies need to make some sharp distinctions between those who are a part of this community and those who are not. Although we were able to fashion from Rawls's general framework some exceptions to the insulation of these societies, his focus is decidedly domestic.

In this chapter we move in the opposite direction in terms of obligations. Both Peter Singer and Henry Shue argue for duties to aid that transcend national borders. I will do here what I have done previously with Walzer and Rawls; that is, I will address those portions of theory that lend themselves to a discussion of framing an alien admission policy. This is somewhat easier to do with Singer and Shue because their theories are naturally outward looking.

SINGER

Peter Singer throws a great challenge to theorists like Walzer and Rawls. Singer has a very basic premise from which his entire theory of duties to others is built. The stronger version of this theory is "if it is in our power to prevent something bad from happening, without thereby sacrificing anything of comparable moral importance, we ought, morally, to do it."[1] Singer's weaker version is "if it is in our power to prevent something very bad from happening, without sacrificing anything else morally significant, we ought, morally, to do it."[2] His well-known example is that of a child drowning in a nearby shallow pond.[3] Singer asserts that saving this child is more important than whether the would-be lifesaver gets muddy. From this intuitive example Singer builds his edifice. Singer dismisses the argument that aid should first go to compatriots, or even to members of one's own family quite generally. "Ethics does not demand that we eliminate personal relationships and partial affections, but it does demand that when we act we assess the moral claims of those affected by our actions independently of our feelings for them."[4]

It is quite possible to incorporate Singer's utilitarian theory of aiding others into an alien admission system. Here alien admissions would be a part of a larger plan to aid others. The overriding feature of such a policy would be to promote human welfare, particularly to save human life.[5] In other words, you do not admit individuals just because they happen to have family members in receiving societies, or because of certain manpower shortages, but you would admit certain individuals because these people are dying or suffering terribly and, by admitting these individuals to your country, you help to save them from such fates.

The alien admission system that I develop in Part II is premised on this notion that helping those who are in serious need should be the primary goal of a nation's alien admission system. That is, I believe that Singer is correct: helping those in serious need *is* more important than virtually any other action that individuals could take. What I attempt to do in Part II is to make this analysis sharper, and I try to do this by placing certain duties on particular societies.

The common charge against Singer's theory is that it knows no bounds in terms of giving aid. To use alien admissions as an example, it could be argued that countless millions from destitute or war-torn countries would increase their happiness (and world happiness in general) by migrating to a country like the United States.[6] In the short run, this argument of increased marginal utility would seem to prompt a utilitarian to advocate greatly increased migration by the destitute and persecuted to some haven. If we took a more long-run view, however, the massive migration of individuals to other societies might not in fact increase total utility.

The better reasoned utilitarian approach would be a rule utilitarian perspective. Under this view, we would try to establish an alien admission system that would maximize utility in the long run. I would suggest that the alien admission system that would emerge would be one where communities are generally left free to develop in their own ways. In this way individuals within those societies would have a greater sense of individual autonomy and control. This is not to say that no individuals would be admitted to other societies. To the contrary, alien admissions could be a very useful means of increasing utility. What such a system seeks to guard against, however, is the admission of such overwhelming numbers that individuals living in these communities completely lose their sense of autonomy and purpose. That is, frequent, large-scale migrations of people would ultimately bring about a sharp decline in total utility, but a small-scale, controlled alien admission practice would not.

Another reason why a rule utilitarian would seek to limit alien admissions is that the evidence indicates that greater numbers of individuals could be assisted with forms of aid other than alien admission. Charles Keely[7] has argued this point in his work on the relationship between refugee flows and political development.[8] Keely's point is that there is a direct connection between political development and refugee flows, and that by admitting refugees from developing nations you are often treating the symptom rather than the cause. He argues that "a given amount of money spent on a development approach will do more to relieve human suffering and advance permanent solutions for the bulk of today's refugees than the same amount of money spent on third-country resettlement."⁹ Because in many instances aid will reach more individuals than alien admissions, utility will be maximized through the former rather than the latter.

SHUE

Henry Shue is another theorist who takes a decidedly nontraditional view of the nation-state. This is not to say that nation-states are irrelevant in his scheme; however, in his theory they are not to demarcate how far our moral obligations reach.[10] Singer arrives at his theory by utilitarian means, while Shue presents a rights-based theory.

Basic Rights

Henry Shue argues that all individuals have certain basic rights, defined this way:

> Basic rights are a restraint upon economic and political forces that would otherwise be too strong to be resisted. They are social guarantees against actual and threatened deprivations of at least some basic needs. Basic rights are an attempt to give the powerless a veto over some of the forces that would otherwise harm them the most.... Basic rights are the morality of the depths. They specify the line beneath which no one is to be allowed to sink.[11]

Shue sets forth three basic rights: security rights, subsistence rights, and the right to liberty (which, as Shue describes it, turns into a right to participate in the process of governing in one's society). On one level, Shue's ideas about basic rights would fit quite logically into a coherent and manageable alien admission system. Shue argues that subsistence rights can be met through foreign assistance. Therefore, alien admissions would not be an integral part of meeting this right. The third basic right, the right to participate in the process of governing, would be unrelated to alien admissions. That is, many nations in the world deny their citizens the right to participate in the process of governing that society. Surely Shue would not advocate admitting individuals simply on the basis of being denied a right that literally millions of people are denied. On the other hand, the first basic right, the right to security, blends quite nicely with an alien admission system. Those who were being tortured or persecuted by others could have their basic rights met by migrating to societies where they would be free from such physical and psychological harm.

Of Shue's three basic rights, two are substantive (security, subsistence), and the other one is procedural (right to participate). Shue argues that the right to participate is an essential right because without it the other two basic rights (and all other rights that flow from these two basic rights) would be in jeopardy:

> It is not possible to enjoy full rights to security or to subsistence without also having rights to participate effectively in the control of security and subsistence. A right is the basis for a certain kind of demand; a demand the fulfillment of which ought to be socially guaranteed. Without channels through which the demand can be made known to those who ought to be guaranteeing its fulfillment, when it is in fact being ignored, one cannot exercise the right.[12]

Shue's premise is that participation in the governing of one's society would somehow matter, at least to some degree, in determining whether the rights of subsistence and security are met. This assumes too much. Other nations, or multinational corporations from other nations, may have a more profound influence on whether the basic rights of citizens in foreign lands are protected than the host government. Shue recognizes as much in his article, "Exporting Hazards." Participation in one's own government, in many instances, will neither be a necessary or sufficient condition for the protection of substantive basic rights. I conclude that although the right to participate in the governing of one's society is an important right, it is not as basic as the right to subsistence and the right to security.

The right to subsistence also needs a closer look. Shue explains it this way:

> But the basic idea is to have available for consumption what is needed for a decent chance at a reasonably healthy and active life of more or

less normal length, barring tragic interventions. This central idea is clear enough to work with, even though disputes can occur over exactly where to draw its outer boundaries. A right to subsistence would not mean, at one extreme, that every baby born with a need for open-heart surgery has a right to have it, but it would also not count as adequate food a diet that produces a life expectancy of 35 years of fever-laden, parasite-ridden listlessness.[13]

To use Shue's example, it is not clear why a right to subsistence would not require that we meet the needs of children who need open-heart surgery. If one was quite serious about rights, then this would not seem to be an "extreme" position at all. Arguments for national health care in this country are drawn exactly along the lines that individuals have a right to certain medical attention, such as open-heart surgery. Shue limits the scope of this right by speaking of "standard threats." I am not convinced that this greatly advances understanding in this murky area. Some might choose to view "standard" in a very broad fashion, others might take a very restrictive view. What was once considered to be quite exotic medical treatment is now standard fare. Shue himself seems to take a halfway measure. The point is that from the language quoted above, it begins to sound as if Shue's theory is not really speaking of a basic right to subsistence as much as it is saying that individuals should not have to live under intolerable conditions. Although this might seem to be a slight distinction, it is important to be concise about the rights that are to be protected. To conclude, Shue's notion of a basic right to subsistence could be stronger. The practical effect of this is that the sacrifice called for is not as far-ranging as it might be.

Duties

Shue makes a major advance in theory by considering different types of duties. His tripartite theory of duties is: (I) the duty not to deprive, (II) the duty to protect, and (III) the duty to give aid. The second duty has two parts: (1) to enforce duty I, and (2) to design institutions that avoid the creation of strong incentives to violate duty I. The third duty is divided up into (1) aid to those who are one's responsibility, (2) aid to victims of social failure in the performance of duties, and (3) aid to victims of natural disasters.[14]

This model of duties begins to break down when it comes to determining who has what duty, for what reasons, and what the extent of these duties are. The clearest duty is the first duty, the duty not to deprive others. This obligates everyone—the individual, the corporation, the nation—and at all times. The basis for part 1 of duty III is also fairly clear. Shue talks about certain relationships, such as family relationships, that will obligate individuals to care for one another.[15] Shue uses the example of parents caring for their young children, or children caring for their aged parents. Other than these two duties, Shue's analysis becomes less than clear. Shue states that "every basic right entails duties of all three types."[16] However, Shue also goes on to state, "This by no means implies, as I have already mentioned, that all three types of duties fall upon everyone else or even fall equally upon everyone upon whom they do fall."[17]

The problem with Shue's analysis is that it is impossible to determine just where these duties would in fact lie. To show this, I will use Shue's example of the Dutch agricultural export policy in Java that has had disastrous results in that country.[18] Shue sees this as a "Sisyphean duty" which falls "to some degree upon the Dutch people who are today still profiting from their centuries of spoils."[19] To confront the issue directly, why are the Dutch only responsible "to some degree?" It would seem clear from Shue's description that there is a causal link between Dutch action and the destitution of the citizens of Java. Shue's response, however, is quite indeterminate: "But whoever precisely has these duties to aid—there are plenty to go around—their magnitude has already been multiplied by past deriliction in the performance of the other two kinds of duties by the Dutch, among others."[20]

By positing that there are plenty of duties to go around, Shue is essentially saying that there are duties out there but we cannot be much more specific than that. The better reasoned view is given by Walzer,[21] who argues that it is essential that moral obligations be limited (and presumably well specified), or else individuals will ignore them because of the lack of specificity, or individuals will simply be overwhelmed by such obligations.[22]

Although Shue makes an attempt to specify what actions prompt what duties, as he begins to advance his theory in *Basic Rights* his analysis of duties becomes looser. At one point he writes:

> given that everyone has a right to subsistence, and that every right to subsistence includes a duty to aid, who have the duties to aid? And the answer suggested is: at least the affluent, characterized as those consuming the absolutely largest amounts for the satisfaction of mere preferences (their own or other people's).[23]

In terms of the amount of aid to be given, Shue writes:

> How much any given individual or nation would in fact need to sacrifice in order for those deprived of subsistence in fact to enjoy the subsistence to which they have rights clearly depends upon the extent to which the rest of whoever ought to make some sacrifices make the sacrifices they ought to make.[24]

Finally, Shue eventually takes a stand that is strikingly similar to Singer's. "One is required to sacrifice, as necessary, anything but one's basic rights in order to honor the basic rights of others."[25] Shue does not think that those in affluent societies would ever have to sacrifice nearly this much. While this is debatable, the philosophical point is more interesting to note.

What seems to have happened to Shue's notion of duties is that it eventually becomes impossible to lodge moral responsibility with specific individuals or nations. Instead of providing a clear analysis for what actions are necessary to prompt certain duties, Shue eventually takes the opposite approach. Duties begin to fall more on "the affluent" quite generally, rather than on any particular members of this class. Moreover, the level of one's moral responsibilities fluctuates depending on what other nations happen to do. I think this picture of moral duties is an incorrect one; in fact, what ultimately emerges from Shue's notion of duties are really not duties as such because they are so open-ended.

Instead of leaving duties as open-ended as Shue has, I think there is a slightly different way of viewing Shue's theory that would remove a great deal of uncertainty as to who has what duty. I think it would be possible, and quite consistent with his general aims, to see the duty not to deprive as a more basic duty than the duty to protect and the duty to aid. For one thing, Shue is quite clear that the duty not to deprive falls on everyone and at all times. From this, all of those who have breached this duty not to deprive would be obligated under the duty to protect and the duty to aid. Shue seems to be suggesting something similar to this in his discussion of the Dutch duty to Java, but if this is his position it is timidly drawn. This notion of having a special duty to protect and aid those we have harmed is the basis for the Harm Principle which I discuss at length in Part II. This is not to say that only those who have breached the first duty will have the second and third duty. In Part II I will talk about a duty to aid that is not based on violating the duty not to deprive. This is what I term the Basic Rights Principle. This duty is not as strong as the duty under the Harm Principle because it is not based on the notion of having deprived others.

A closer analysis of the duty to protect is also needed. It is not readily apparent from Shue's theory what would prompt this particular duty. I suggest that those who would definitely have this duty would be those who put themselves in a position where they might deprive others of their basic rights. War is the clearest example. All nations have a duty not to harm civilians in other societies. This is simply the duty not to deprive. However, some nations will have a special duty of protection, namely those nations that are involved in the war. Unlike nonintervening nations, those who participate in a war in another country have placed themselves in a position where they could quite easily cause serious harm to noncombatants. Under duty I these nations have a general duty not to deprive. However, I argue that they must do more than this. They must also protect. That is, because they have placed themselves in a position where they might do great harm, they must take special measures above and beyond the duty of nonintervening nations to ensure that they do not deprive.

CONCLUSION

In this chapter I have considered two theorists who argue that we must look beyond national borders in terms of giving aid to others in need. Singer presents a consequentialist argument. In essence he argues that promoting human welfare is more important than virtually any other action that individuals could take. As a result, the alien admission system that I see emerging from Singer's theory would be one that places a premium on helping those who are in serious need. To the possible argument that Singer's notion of aid knows no bounds, I have argued from a rule utilitarian perspective that total utility would be maximized in the long run where efforts were made to help those in dire need, but where the autonomy of communities was also protected.

Shue presents a rights-based theory, but he arrives at conclusions similar to Singer's. On one level Shue's theory lends itself quite nicely to framing an alien admission policy. What I have done in the preceding pages, however, is to question the legitimacy of some of Shue's claims about the basic rights that he presents. I have argued that the right to participate is not as basic as the right to subsistence and security. I have also questioned whether Shue really does mean to say that individuals have a right to subsistence, or if he means to say that those who are in serious need should receive aid. I find the qualifier "standard threats" devoid of any real meaning. Standard to whom? Standard to what society? The need to be more concise in this analysis would be more evident if Shue had not downplayed the amount of aid that might be needed to meet this basic right to subsistence.[26]

Shue's notion of varying duties marks an important advance in philosophical thought. In a number of instances, however, there is too much uncertainty in terms of who has what duty and for what reasons. This is a shortcoming that by no means seriously detracts from the thrust of his arguments. I spend most of Part II trying to build from Shue's base. The reader is left to judge whether the responsibility for certain duties is specified with any greater certainty.

NOTES

1. Peter Singer, "Famine, Affluence, and Morality," *Philosophy and Public Affairs* 1 (1972): 231.
2. Ibid., 235.
3. Ibid., 231.
4. Peter Singer, *Practical Ethics* (Cambridge: Cambridge University Press, 1979), 67.
5. One issue that I do not address here is whether we have a duty to save the lives of animals too. I prefer to avoid this issue. See Singer's thoughts in *Animal Liberation* (New York: New York Review, 1975).
6. In remarks inserted into the *Congressional Record*, Congressman Les Aspin argues that "polls show that two out of every three people in Latin America would come here if they could." *Cong. Rec.* Sept. 5, 1980, E.4232. I am unaware of what polls Mr. Aspin is referring to. My intuitive feeling, however, is that given the present condition in many countries, large numbers of people would quite naturally want to migrate to a country like the United States. It is by no means apparent, however, that absent these terrible conditions very many people would want to leave their own communities.
7. Charles Keely, *Global Refugee Policy: The Case for a Development-Oriented Strategy* (New York: Population Council, 1981).
8. For other discussions of this relationship see Richard Hofstetter, "Economic Underdevelopment and the Population Explosion: Implications for U.S. Immigration Policy," *Law and Contemporary Problems* 45 (1982): 55–79. Sidney Weintraub, "Illegal Immigration and U.S. Foreign Economic Policy," in Demetrious Papademetriou and Mark Miller, eds., *The Unavoidable Issue: U.S. Immigration Policy in the 1980's* (Philadelphia: Institute for the Study of Human Issues, 1983).
9. Keely, *Global Refugee Policy*, 23.
10. Although there are many similarities between someone like Charles Beitz and Henry Shue, I focus my attention on Shue.
11. Henry Shue, *Basic Rights: Subsistence, Affluence, and U.S. Foreign Policy* (Princeton: Princeton University Press, 1980), 18.
12. Ibid., 75.
13. Ibid., 23.
14. Ibid., 60.
15. It is unclear to me whether this duty would prompt Shue's theory to base alien admissions along family reunification grounds. Shue has gone on public record against the forced separation of families under the proposed legalization provisions of the Simpson-Mazzoli bill. See

U.S. Cong., House, Hearings before the Subcommittee on Immigration, Refugees, and International Law of the Committee on the Judiciary, *Hearings on Immigration*, 97th Cong., 1st sess., Oct. 14, 1981, 31. One argument against Shue being able to take a stand promoting family reunification quite generally in our immigration system is that such assistance to family members might take the place of aiding others. It should be quite evident that this comparison of claims is one of the basic points that I stress here, and one reason why I think our moral choices are indeed much more difficult than most, including Shue, would have them.

16. Shue, *Basic Rights*, 53.
17. Ibid.
18. Ibid., 63.
19. Ibid.
20. Ibid.
21. See chapter 1.
22. A. I. Melden has similarly argued that those who have infringed on the rights of others must be made aware of that fact in the strongest terms. See A. I. Melden, *Rights and Persons* (Berkeley: University of California Press, 1977), 173.
23. Shue, *Basic Rights*, 120.
24. Ibid., 118.
25. Ibid., 114.
26. For an argument that sees a great deal of sacrifice needed if we are to meet the challenge of meeting the subsistence needs of others, see Garrett Hardin, "Lifeboat Ethics: The Case Against Helping the Poor," in William Aiken and Hugh LaFollette, eds., *World Hunger and Moral Obligations* (Englewood Cliffs, N.J.: Prentice-Hall, 1977).

Chapter 4
Bruce Ackerman

One of the few theorists to directly address the question of alien admissions is Bruce Ackerman in his book *Social Justice in the Liberal State*.[1] As I mentioned in the Introduction, it is difficult to categorize Ackerman as either working within the traditional notion of the nation-state or not. Ackerman calls for a prima facie right to migrate, but at the same time he talks about maintaining a communal process within a liberal state. In this chapter I examine each of these portions of his theory to see if they are theoretically compatible, particularly as Ackerman presents them.

THE ALIEN DIALOGUES

The first time that Ackerman treats alien admissions he does so in a dialogue between Explorer and Apollonian.[2] The hypothetical situation that Ackerman uses is one in which Explorer and Apollo are two spaceships on a discovery voyage. Both come upon an unclaimed planet at the same time, but Explorer lands on this planet slightly ahead of Apollo. The citizens on board the Explorer claim all of the manna (Ackerman's term for social goods) on this planet, but the citizens of Apollo demand justification for why the Explorers should be able to possess all of the manna. Under Ackerman's scheme, individuals must respond to such questions,[3] and they must be consistent in their responses to different questioners.[4] In addition, Ackerman's concept of neutrality requires that individuals cannot assert that their conception of the good is better than anybody else's, or that they are intrinsically superior to any other fellow citizen.[5]

Ackerman comments this way on the Apollonian-Explorer dialogue:

Quite unthinkingly, we have come to accept the idea that we have the right to exclude nonresidents from our midst. Yet, unless something further can be said, the dialogue between Explorer and Appollonian applies equally to the conversation between a rich American and an impoverished Mexican who swims over the border for a talk. The American can no more declare the intrinsic superiority of the first occupant than the Explorer can. Instead, it is only a very strong empirical claim that can permit the American to justify exclusion of the foreign-born from "his" liberal state.[6]

Ackerman then employs a second dialogue to represent a real world example. This dialogue is between Westerner, who symbolizes rich, liberal societies, and Easterner, who represents poorer societies and/or those who are ruled by an "authoritarian dictatorship in which a small elite explicitly declares its superiority over the masses they exploit."[7] Ackerman posits a situation where the West has adopted a forthcoming policy admitting a large number—Z—of Easterners on a first come, first served basis. Ackerman also sets the scene by positing that Z is so large that it strains the capacity of Western institutions to sustain a liberal political conversation. Finally, Ackerman hypothesizes if the West takes in any more aliens past Z the presence of so many newcomers will cause a fascist dictatorship to take control of the government in the West.[8]

The conversation, then, is between those Easterners past the Z cutoff who want to be admitted to the West and the West itself.

EASTERNER: I demand recognition as a citizen of this liberal state.
WESTERN STATESMAN: We refuse.

EASTERNER: What gives you the right to refuse me? Do you think I would fail to qualify as a citizen of an ideal liberal state?

WESTERNER: Not at all.

EASTERNER: Do you imagine you're better than me simply because you've been born west of this frontier?

WESTERNER: No. If that were all, I would not hesitate before admitting you.

EASTERNER: Well, then, what's the trouble?

WESTERNER: The fact is that we in the West are far from achieving a perfect technology of justice; if we admit more than Z newcomers, our existing institutions will be unable to function in anything but an explicitly authoritarian manner.

EASTERNER: But why am I being asked to bear the costs of imperfection?

WESTERNER: Sorry, we're doing everything we can. But Z is the limit of immigrants.

EASTERNER: But you're not doing *everything*. Why not expel some of your native-born Westerners and make room for me? Do you think they're better than I am?

WESTERNER: Z is the limit of our assimilative capacity only on the assumption that there exists a cadre of natives familiar with the operation of liberal institutions. If some of the natives were removed from the population, even Z would be too many.

EASTERNER: So what am I to do? I'll be dead before I get to the front of the line of immigrants.

WESTERNER: Go back to your own people and build your own liberal state. We'll try to help you out as best we can.[9]

Ackerman calls this a "hard" conversation, and concludes that there may in fact be little hope that a liberal conversation can be built in the East. However, he thinks that this is the best that can be achieved in the "real world." Ackerman then concludes: "The *only* reason for restricting immigration is to protect the ongoing process of liberal conversation itself. Can our present immigration practices be rationalized on this ground?"[10]

THE LIBERAL STATE

The first issue I want to address with regard to Ackerman's views on alien admissions is how he views the nature of the state itself. If we back up to the first dialogue, notice that Ackerman is not talking about a situation where a group of individuals have lived on a planet for centuries and then an outside group seeks to move in on "their" community. Instead, Ackerman presents a situation that would, quite naturally I think, lead one to say that the manna on the planet should somehow be shared. After all, Explorer barely arrived sooner than Apollo. Even the fact that Ackerman talks about sharing manna, rather than creating or invading communities, is noteworthy. If Ackerman had presented the "other" kind of fact situation—one where individuals had lived in a community for quite a long period of time, where there was sharing and caring between members, and where the riches of the community resulted from the efforts of its members—then I would think most people would not be so quick to honor the claims of most latecomers.

Although Ackerman's stated purpose is to justify the existence of the liberal state, in many respects Ackerman has a very different and weaker sense of the role that communities play in our lives than either Walzer or Rawls.[11] Toward the end of his book Ackerman writes:

> Rather than achieving his sense of individuality independently of the political community, each citizen of a liberal state begins his encounter with his fellows with the most naive kind of self assertion: "I want it, what gives you the right to deprive me of it?" It is only by trying to talk about this question that you and I gradually gain a sense of the rightful spheres in which each of us may assert our individuality.[12]

A short while later Ackerman says this about his liberal society and the apparent lack of caring and sharing or love between members:

> What is forged instead [of love] is a bond that ties citizens together without forcing them to be brothers; liberal conversation provides a communal process that deepens each person's claim to autonomy at the same time that he recognizes others as no less worthy of respect.[13]

What is not clear is how the liberal conversation creates this communal feeling, or how it could be considered a communal process as such. The "liberal conversation" itself is oftentimes little more than individuals asserting their own claims to social goods and challenging those put forth by others. Beyond that, the liberal conversation essentially deals only with one portion of community and that is how social goods are distributed. That is, in a Walzerian or Rawlsian community individuals share both social goods and political power. The two are interrelated. In Ackerman's theory, on the other hand, the citizens of the liberal state really never get around to discussing anything but the distribution of goods. In addition, it is difficult to understand how individuals within each society truly do share in the lives of other members of that society. What points this out quite vividly is the fact that the conversation between fellow members is no different from the conversation between East and West: demands are made and responses to these demands are provided. If the liberal dialogue itself helps to create this communal feeling, as Ackerman suggests, then perhaps we would expect a comparable feeling to arise between the East and West, yet we know that Ackerman does not envision this.

Against this position, it might be argued that the end product of the liberal conversation is reciprocity, equality, and mutual respect among the members of the community. In other words, individuals begin with egoistic demands, but in the course of the conversation they begin to develop a sense of belonging with others in a community. In terms of political power, Ackerman's response would probably be that the same principles that govern the exchange of goods in a society could be extended to cover the distribution of political power as well.

What casts strong doubt on this response is where Ackerman draws the line on alien admissions. The Z cutoff is perilously close to a takeover by a fascist mob. I think this goes much too far. The fact that societies are pushed to open their borders to this point is an indication that a great deal of the autonomy of these communities has already been lost. In previous chapters I spoke about the need to allow communities to freely develop on their own. Ackerman's cutoff point would not allow this process to occur.

As a side issue to all of this, it is noteworthy that Ackerman seems to make little differentiation in terms of whom we should admit. In his East-West example, the West accepted Easterners because these people came from poor countries, or from countries with unjust regimes. Apparently Ackerman thinks that each of these kinds of individuals would be equally deserving of admission. What this does not take into consideration is that citizens past the Z mark might be even poorer and have suffered even more persecution than those who have been admitted. In fact, Ackerman seems to presume that all of those who live in poor and unjust regimes will suffer the same, although I do not think this is by any means an accurate account. Ackerman's alien admission system opens itself up to the same kinds of problems that exist under the current brain drain phenomenon. That is, although Ackerman's goal is to help those in poor countries (to use this example), his alien admission policy might result in making the East and those who live there even poorer, particularly if those who migrate are the ones with capital to invest, or if they happen to be the intelligentsia of the society.

Another instance where Ackerman's theory would not properly protect liberal societies is his description of foreign assistance. At first Ackerman speaks about India and China "demanding" billions of dollars so that they could construct a liberal dialogue (as if money were the only prerequisite). Ackerman writes:

To refuse such a demand, the rich people of the world would be obliged to respond in a plainly exploitative fashion. They would be forced to say that they were entitled to more simply because they were born on one side of an arbitrary geographic boundary rather than another, that Americans were intrinsically superior to Indians, Japanese to Chinese.[14]

Ackerman then goes on to say that such a result might make us all starve together. To avoid this end, Ackerman backtracks and talks about a substantial aid program, but one which is limited to "underdeveloped countries of a liberal tendency."[15] What seems to concern Ackerman, then, is not the possible harm to communities that such demands might cause. Instead, his primary concern seems to be starvation. What he seems to be saying is that aid must be given up to the point where "we" would all starve together. I qualify Ackerman's concern for preventing starvation because he seems to worry about such an occurrence only in countries of a liberal tendency. One possible explanation is that Ackerman might mean that assistance to unjust regimes might be meaningless because the government in power would confiscate such aid. Again, it is not clear why aid is limited to countries of a liberal tendency. In any event, the more important point is that Ackerman professes to be concerned with the protection of the liberal state, but his theory calls for a number of phenomena that would have disastrous consequences for many communities.

CONCLUSION

As I noted in the Introduction, Ackerman is a difficult philosopher to classify. In some respects he is a traditionalist in the sense that he concerns himself with maintaining a political community—the liberal state. In many other respects Ackerman is anything but a traditionalist. The most obvious example of this is his claim that aliens have a prima facie right to admission. Ackerman states: The *only* reason for restricting immigration is to protect the ongoing process of liberal conversation itself. Can our present immigration practices be rationalized on this ground? Although alien admission practices can be an essential means of meeting the basic rights of others, Ackerman's approach goes too far.

I have pointed out here that Ackerman's original dialogue between Explorer and Apollonian is inherently biased for two reasons: (1) because of the fact situation that has Explorer getting to the unclaimed planet moments before Apollo, and (2) because Ackerman talks about social goods (manna) rather than about actual communities. The inconsistencies in Ackerman's treatment of protecting liberal communities, but at the same time honoring the claims of strangers, is a good indication of how intractable these two goals might be. It is a problem that has faced every philosopher examined thus far, to one degree or another. What I will do in Part II is make an effort to draw the balance between these two goals better than it has been drawn thus far.

NOTES

1. Bruce Ackerman, *Social Justice in the Liberal State* (New Haven: Yale University Press, 1980).
2. Ibid., chapter 3.
3. Ibid., 4. This is Ackerman's rationality principle, the idea that whenever anyone questions the legitimacy of another's power the power holder must respond not by suppressing the questioner, but by giving a reason why he is more entitled to the resource than the questioner is.
4. Ibid., 7. This is Ackerman's consistency principle, the reason advanced by a power wielder on one occasion must not be inconsistent with the reasons he advances to justify his other claims to power.
5. Ibid., 11.
6. Ibid., 93.
7. Ibid.
8. It is never clear how this Z figure would be arrived at, or how policymakers would know they were reaching a point where a fascist takeover was likely to occur. A lot might depend on the kinds of people who are admitted. For example, the population of the West would certainly be more frustrated by the admission of rabble-rousers than they would be if those granted admission were ideological allies or family members.
9. Ibid., 94.
10. Ibid., 95.
11. Ibid., 30. "By the end of our imaginary journey, we shall glimpse a world that is committed both to individual rights and democratic decision; that uses the power of government to strike at the roots of exploitation while remaining conscious of the dangers of bureaucratic tyranny. In short, our commitment to Neutral dialogue has led us to a familiar form of policy—the liberal-democratic welfare state.... The contemporary liberal state will no longer seem a random jumble of ideas tossed up by a century-long conflict between the partisans of Locke and Marx...."
12. Ibid., 346.
13. Ibid., 347.
14. Ibid., 256.
15. Ibid., 257.

Chapter 5
Community in America

THE SEARCH FOR COMMUNITY

It has been in the context of alien admissions that the concept of an autonomous American political community has often been expressed, for better or for worse. Even if most matters of the day are not explicitly premised on this idea of community, the area of alien admissions seems driven by it.[1] On a very basic level, the various grounds for exclusion and deportation are a clear indication that we only wish to admit certain kinds of people for membership in this community.[2]

Yet "community" has not only been defined by qualities that individuals possess, but also by determinations that certain groups of people do not fit within the "American community." The following is a lengthy but instructive passage from one of the earliest alien admission cases decided by the Supreme Court. In this opinion the Court is upholding a statute which served to exclude Chinese laborers from this country.[3] The underlying rationale for the decision and for Congressional policy appears this way:

The differences in race added greatly to the difficulties of the situation. Notwithstanding the favorable provisions of the new articles of the

Treaty of 1868, by which all the privileges, immunities, and exemptions were extended to subjects of China in the United States which were accorded to citizens or subjects of the most favored nation, they remained strangers in the land, residing apart by themselves, and adhering to the customs and usages of their own country. It seemed impossible for them to assimilate with our people or to make any change in their habits or modes of living. As they grew in numbers each year the people of the coast saw, or believed they saw, in the facility of immigration, and in the crowded millions of China, where population presses upon the means of subsistence, great danger that at no distant day that portion of our country would be overrun by them unless prompt action was taken to restrict their immigration. The people there accordingly petitioned earnestly for protective legislation.[4]

With hindsight readily available, it is too easy to scoff at such fears of an unassimilated "yellow horde." No doubt there were many factors at work, among them the fact that Chinese laborers posed a very real threat to the livelihood of native workers. In addition, some very educated people believed in the natural superiority of the white race. What needs to be balanced off against the views that our present knowledge offers is the fact that large groups of strangers in our midst might be a disruptive or destabilizing force in many communities. What is difficult to do is to ferret out the real fears from those based on hyperbole and illusions.

The fears of 100 years ago are still present.[5] The same kinds of concerns for protecting "the American community" still lie at the base of current alien admission proposals. The following is from the Senate Report of the Simpson-Mazzoli legislation, Congress' latest attempt to tackle immigration reform:

If immigration is continued at a high level, yet a substantial portion of these new persons and their descendants do not assimilate into the society, they have the potential to create in America a measure of the same social, political, and economic problems which exist in the countries from which they have chosen to depart. Furthermore, if language and cultural separatism rise above a certain level, the unity and political stability of the nation will—in time—be seriously diminished. Pluralism, within a united American nation, has been the single greatest strength of this country. This unity comes from a common language and a core public culture of certain shared values, beliefs, and customs which make us distinctly "Americans."[6]

In his masterful work on U.S. immigration policy, John Higham talks about two national characteristics that seem to coexist at the same time that they are in direct conflict. One characteristic is the idea of the United States as the home of immigrants, reflecting that oft-quoted language inscribed on the Statue of Liberty. This has been no mere image. This nation has not only been a home for immigrants in the past, as is it has so often been depicted, but it is still very much a home for aliens at the present time. In fact, if illegal aliens are included in our calculations we might be seeing the highest alien admissions totals ever, in absolute numbers.[7] Juxtaposed against this characteristic is the other national characteristic: a nativist streak that has displayed itself at various times in U.S. history. The language from the Chinese Exclusion Case reflects this characteristic, and to a large extent this point of view is still very much in evidence today.[8]

THE DEVELOPMENT OF COMMUNITY BY THE JUDICIARY

In this section I consider the role the courts have played in helping to determine the concept of "community" in this country. Why focus on the courts? Peter Schuck has recently written that, "Because it was Congress that essentially shaped the legal dimensions of the national community, its contours reflected the parochial, temporal political values so characteristic of the legislative process rather than the more cosmopolitan values of universality and pluralism."[9] The tacit assumption is that a more active stance by the judicial branch would have avoided some of our past racist immigration standards, and also some of our deplorable treatment of aliens lawfully admitted to this country.

Kenneth Karst has similarly suggested that legislatures mainly serve as brokerage houses for individualistic exchange, while courts represent our community values.[10] Whether the courts, historically, have in fact represented this nation's "better" or more humanistic side is open to question, as we will soon see.

However, Karst's comments seem much more on point in recent U.S. history.[11] The concept of "community" has been an evolving concept, and the judicial branch is now beginning to play an integral role in its definition.

Initial Entry/Deportation/Reentry

In matters of initial entry the judicial branch has displayed a remarkable deference to the political branches. In one of the earliest cases before the Supreme Court the Court stated:

> The question whether, and upon what conditions, these aliens shall be permitted to remain within the United States being one to be determined by the political departments of the government, the judicial department cannot properly express an opinion upon the wisdom, the policy or the justice of the measures enacted by Congress in the exercise of the powers confided to it by the Constitution over this subject.[12]

The Court watched inertly[13] as Asians were excluded and the entry of other undesirables was restricted.[14] Even with the abandonment of the national origins quota system in 1965, the Court maintained the position that the decision to admit was not one for it to make.[15]

Throughout the course of the last decade the Supreme Court has remained entirely consistent with its previous holdings. For example, the Court employed this language in *Fiallo v. Bell*[16], a case involving the question whether the Congress could allow mothers and illegitimate children to be considered "immediate relatives," but not fathers and their illegitimate children: "At the outset, it is important to underscore the limited scope of judicial inquiry into immigration legislation. This Court has repeatedly emphasized that over no conceivable subject is the legislative power of Congress more complete than it is over the admission of aliens."[17] In terms of initial entry, then, the Supreme Court has acceded to the determination of the political branches which strangers were to become members.[18] That is also to say that the Court has underlined the old concept of a nation's (but read political branches') absolute right to control its borders.

The members-strangers dichotomy has a limited function here, however, because the Court has also given more attention to aliens who are beginning to look as much like members as strangers. For example, in the area of deportation, aliens who are in the United States, whether legally or illegally, have been afforded more procedural and substantive rights than those seeking initial entry.[19] Moreover, this eventual recognition[20] of the importance of having lived in this country has, at times, been prompted by the judicial branch itself.[21]

One of the previous anomalies in this area was that aliens who had lived in this country, but who had then left for short periods of time, were treated as strangers when they attempted to reenter the United States.[22] However, in recent years the Court has made incursions into the legislative standard of "entry" that reflects the alien's past ties to the U.S. community.[23]

For example, in *Rosenberg v. Fleuti* the Court began in earnest to carve out an exception to the statutory rule.[24] In this case the resident alien had been living in the United States for four years, but had then gone to Mexico for "a couple of hours." Judicial precedent, and even legislative intent, would have dictated a summary exclusion of this alien, notwithstanding his former residence in this country. However, the Court held that this trip did not constitute a "meaningful interruption" of the alien's residence here. The *Fleuti* exception was further strengthened in 1982 in *Landon v. Plascencia*.[25] Here the resident alien's departure from the U.S. lasted several days, and Plascencia was arrested attempting to smuggle in illegal aliens when she attempted to return. The alien claimed that the proper action was a deportation hearing rather than an exclusion, but the Supreme Court disagreed. What the Court did do, however, was to recognize the importance of the alien's past ties to this community: "once an alien gains admission to our country and begins to develop the ties that go with permanent residence, his constitutional status changes accordingly."[26]

To summarize, although the Supreme Court has played a deferential role to the political branches in terms of which strangers should be admitted to the country, the Court is not willing to play this same role when the question involves aliens who have lived and worked in our midst. The Court is now recognizing that for those individuals who are already in this country, a sharp distinction between members and strangers cannot justifiably be made.

The Bifurcation of Community

Perhaps the Court's treatment of lawfully admitted resident aliens who live and work (or try to work) here is even more instructive in terms of how community and notions of membership have been defined. As a general rule, resident aliens have had a long history of being discriminated against (in a descriptive if not pejorative sense). Most of this discrimination has come from individual states, and for a long period of time the Supreme Court kept a hands-off approach to such legislation. The examples of discrimination against aliens upheld by the Supreme Court are legion. The Court has allowed individual states to treat aliens differently from citizens in a wide range of activities, ranging from denying aliens the right to operate billiard halls and to possess liquor licenses, to prohibiting them from owning land.[27] The one exception to this was that the Court seemed unwilling to defer to a state's will when efforts were made to prevent resident aliens from earning a livelihood quite generally.[28]

Since the 1960s, however, the Court has taken a much more critical view of statutes that singled out aliens for disparate treatment. Perhaps the height of Supreme Court involvement occurred in *Graham v. Richardson*, where the Court struck down a state statute making citizenship a prerequisite for welfare.[29] The Court, at that time, enunciated the doctrine that aliens were a "discrete and insular minority," and that classifications according to alienage were to be given the Court's strictest scrutiny.

Since *Graham* the Supreme Court has retreated from this role of defender of the rights of aliens. The Court has quite recently refused to strike down several state statutes that have restricted certain government jobs to citizens. In *Foley v. Connelie* the Court upheld a statute that restricted membership on a state police force to citizens.[30] In *Ambach v. Norwick* the Court likewise refused to strike down a state statute which limited the pool of school teachers to U.S. citizens.[31] Perhaps the most far-reaching case is *Cabell v. Chavez-Salido*, in which the court upheld a California statute which restricted the position of "peace officer" to U.S. citizens, notwithstanding the fact that this was a very broad classification.[32]

The rationale behind the Supreme Court's hesitation here is that the Court views such classifications by the individual states as a valid exercise in preserving the state's own "political community."[33] The Court's decisions in recent years have served to bifurcate the idea of community. Walzer and others speak of a community in terms of a sharing of both economic goods and political power among members. In fact, the two seem complements of one another. The doctrine that seems to be evolving from the Court's decisions, however, is a general division of community into two separate spheres—an economic sphere and a political sphere. Moreover, this division seems to reflect the fact that the Supreme Court is attempting to balance the two competing goals that we will return to quite frequently: the need to maintain the essence of our political communities while at the same time recognizing the basic rights of others.

In the economic sphere, generally, all of those within the physical bounds of the country are to be considered a part of that community. *Graham* stands for this proposition. The one exception to this rule comes in the area of federal discrimination against aliens. For example, in *Matthews v. Diaz* the Court deferred to the political branches of the national government and allowed a federal Medicare classification that distinguished between different classes of resident aliens.[34] The result can be explained on the basis of the longstanding deference to the political branches of the federal government that we discussed previously. However, even this exception might have some severe limitations. In a companion case to *Diaz*, *Hampton v. Mow Sung Wong*,[35] the Court struck down Civil Service regulations restricting government employment to citizens, reasoning that,

The rule enforced by the Commission has its impact on an identifiable class of persons who, entirely apart from the rule itself, are already subject to disadvantages not shared by the remainder of the community. Aliens are not entitled to vote and, as alleged in the complaint, are often handicapped by a lack of familiarity with our language and customs. The added disadvantage resulting from the enforcement of the rule—ineligibility for employment in a major sector of the economy—is of sufficient significance to be characterized as a deprivation of an interest in liberty.[36]

The other community, the political one, is apparently much narrower. Not only are aliens excluded from voting and holding elected political office,[37] but their ability to hold a wide range of governmental positions has been effectively restricted by a number of states.[38] The idea of a narrowly defined political community cannot be taken too far, however. In *Plyler v. Doe* the Supreme Court struck down a Texas statute that authorized local school districts to deny enrollment to children not "legally admitted" into the United States. Although *Plyler* does not fall into line with the Court's other "political community" cases, still, it is a case involving this country's definition of community:

Section 21.031 imposes a lifetime hardship on a discrete class of children not accountable for their disabling status. The stigma of illiteracy will mark them for the rest of their lives. By denying these children a basic education, we deny them the ability to live within the structure of our civic institutions, and foreclose any realistic possibility that they will contribute in even the smallest way to the progress of our Nation.[39]

The *Plyler* case is noteworthy in at least two respects. For one thing it is a frank judicial admission that the old concept of a nation's ability to control its borders, and all of the power that flows from this distinction between members and strangers, might be inapplicable when that nation chooses not to control its borders, or cannot control its borders.[40] *Plyler* seems to suggest that in those instances strangers in our midst should begin to be treated like members for certain purposes. Another noteworthy aspect of *Plyler* is that while other Court decisions have been cognizant of *past* ties with the United States, *Plyler* might stand for the proposition that *future* ties are an important consideration as well.

CONCLUSION

One of the overriding goals of past and present alien admission policy has been the preservation of the U.S. community.

Immigration legislation is currently before the Congress; the often stated assumption behind the legislation is that we have lost control of our national borders; the implicit assumption is that foreigners threaten the autonomy of the American community. Although the preservation of communal autonomy is a vital goal, it also needs to be pointed out that a sharp members-strangers dichotomy is not an accurate portrayal of the larger American community, or many of its subcommunities. The Supreme Court has recently begun to recognize some shadings in the members-strangers distinction. It has also recognized that even if individuals are not an integral part of the political community, their presence here might make them de facto members of the economic community. This country is a community, and it should be preserved as a community; but it is also a relatively open community and it should be recognized as such. Balanced against this goal of preserving our national community is the goal of meeting our moral obligations to individuals in other countries. We now turn to this.

NOTES

1. "The idea of sovereignty, so elusive in our domestic constitutional structure, may come closest to being reified and recognizable when a unified national government deploys its laws against one who is plausibly seen as an outsider—as, quite literally, alien." See Peter Schuck, "The Transformation of Immigration Law," *Columbia Law Review* 84 (1984): 17.

2. See § 212 (a) (1–33), 8 U.S.C. § 1182 (a) (1–33) and Section 241 (a) (1–18) 8 U.S.C. § 1251 (a) (1–18) of the Immigration and Naturalization Act. I think most people not versed in immigration law (which would be most people) would be surprised at the grounds for exclusion, which include: those who are mentally retarded, the insane, homosexuals, drug addicts, paupers, professional beggars or vagrants, individuals convicted of a crime of "moral turpitude," stowaways, prostitutes, polygamists, Communist Party members, and Nazis, to select several provisions. The grounds for deportation are similarly restrictive.

3. One of the ironies of U.S. policy is that it was not until World War II, when China was our ally, that a small quota was established to admit some Chinese nationals.

4. *Chae Chan Ping v. U.S.*, 130 U.S. 581, 595 (1889).

5. One concern is whether aliens who are now coming to this country will become Americans, however that would be defined. One major concern is the degree to which aliens become citizens. In fact, naturalization rates do differ dramatically between various nationalities. For example, the naturalization rates for Asian immigrants is over 80 percent, while it is below 5 percent for both Canadians and Mexicans. U.S. Cong., Senate, Committee on the Judiciary, *Immigration Reform and Control*, Sen. Rept. No. 485, 97th Cong., 2nd sess. (1982), 6.

6. Ibid.

7. For example, in the decade 1910–1920 the average annual number of immigrants admitted to this country was in the vicinity of 800,000. From 1976–1981 normal flow immigration was generally between 400,000 and 600,000. However, if illegal aliens are also considered, the number of aliens coming to this country is probably much greater than at any time in our history. What tempers this is the fact that aliens currently constitute a much smaller percentage of the U.S. population than in earlier times. *U.S. Immigration Policy and the National Interest, Final Report and Recommendations of the Select Commission on Immigration and Refugee Policy*, table 4, p. 92.

8. Teitelbaum points to the very cool reception all incoming aliens currently receive in this country as displayed in public opinion polls. For example, only 19 percent of the American public supported President Carter's decision to double the admission of Indochinese refugees to 168,000, while 46 percent actually wanted a reduction in the previous level of 84,000. In addition 91 percent of the American public support "an all out effort to stop the illegal entry into the United States of 1.5 million foreigners who don't have entry visas." Normal flow immigration does not fare any better. Eighty percent of the public wanted to "reduce the quotas of the number of legal immigrants who can enter into the U.S. every year." See Teitelbaum, "Right Versus Right: Immigration and Refugee Policy in the United States," *Foreign Affairs* 59 (1980): 21. In fact, as Senator Huddleston, one of the most vocal opponents of increased levels of immigration, points out, 65 percent of those polled by the Gallup organization wanted all immigration stopped until unemployment fell below 5 percent. This was further than even Huddleston was willing to push matters. See *Cong. Rec.*, Mar. 24, 1981, S.2579–2583.

9. Schuck, "The Transformation of Immigration Law," 14.

10. Kenneth Karst, "Equality and Community: Lessons from the Civil Rights Era," *Notre Dame Lawyer* 56 (1981): 183.

11. The notion of what constitutes "membership" has changed throughout our history. For example, in *Mackenzie v. Hare*, 239 U.S. 299 (1915), the Court upheld the expatriation of an American citizen for

marrying a British citizen. Similarly, in *Perez v. Brownell*, 356 U.S. 44 (1957), the Court upheld the expatriation of a U.S. citizen who had voted in a foreign election.

12. *Fong Yue Ting v. U.S.*, 149 U.S. 698, 731 (1893). *Fong* was not an "initial entry" case as such, which makes its holding even crueler. The question before the Court in *Fong* was the constitutionality of an act of Congress which provided that lawfully admitted Chinese laborers had to obtain a certificate of residence (proved by at least one white witness) within one year after passage of the Act of May 5, 1892, "An Act to Prohibit the Coming of Chinese Persons into the United States." The Court upheld this legislation.

13. In the majority opinion in *Fong* Justice Gray wrote, "The right of a nation to expel or deport foreigners, who have not been naturalized or taken any steps towards becoming citizens of the country, rests upon the same grounds, and is as absolute and unqualified as the right to prohibit and prevent their entrance into the country." 149 U.S. at 707. In dissent, Justice Brewer used the length of stay in this country to reach an opposite conclusion. "There are 100,000 and more of these persons living in this country, making their homes here, and striving by their labor to earn a livelihood. They are not travelers, but resident aliens." at 734. Brewer went on to comment on the traditional view that nations have absolute control over their borders: "It is said that the power here asserted is inherent in sovereignty. This doctrine of powers inherent in sovereignty is one both indefinite and dangerous. Where are the limits to such powers to be found, and by whom are they to be pronounced?.... The governments of other nations have elastic powers—ours is fixed and bounded by a written constitution." at 737. An equally strong dissent was filed by Justice Field.

14. In 1875 the first qualitative restrictions were passed excluding prostitutes and convicts. The same year that the Chinese were excluded so were lunatics, idiots, and people likely to be public charges. In 1903 political radicals and polygamists were added to the list of those who were to be excluded. In 1907 those with mental and physical defects that might affect their ability to earn a living, as well as those with tuberculosis, were excluded. The list of exclusions has since expanded.

15. One reason put forward by the Court for staying out of this area is that political considerations dominate in the decision of who to exclude. What currently weighs quite heavily against that position is the fact that almost all political considerations were removed with the abandonment of the national origins quota system in 1965. I make this argument in "The Role of the Judiciary in Alien Admissions," *Boston College International and Comparative Law Review* 8 (1985): 341–76.

16. 430 U.S. 787 (1977).

17. 430 U.S. at 792 (cites omitted). It should be noted that as a result there was no family reunification, in this country at least, between such fathers and their illegitimate children.

18. One area where the judicial branch, but really certain lower federal courts, have been much more active in terms of initial entry has been the area of refugee/asylum admissions. The most far ranging case is *Haitian Refugee Center v. Civiletti*, (hereinafter *HRC*) 503 F. Supp. 442 (S.D. Fla., 1980) *aff'd as modified sub nom Haitian Refugee Center v. Smith*, 676 F. 2d 1023 (5th Cir., 1982). In the lower court holding Judge King flatly rejected the findings of a special State Department Study Team, and instead relied on other evidence to conclude that there is indeed persecution in Haiti, and that Haitian boat people should not be sent back to that country. See also *Orantes-Hernandez v. Smith*, 541 F. Supp. 351 (S.D. Calif., 1982); *Fernandez-Roque v. Smith*, 567 F. Supp. 1115 (N.D. Ga., 1983). Whether we are witnessing a trend towards a greater judicial role in initial entry cases, or an erosion of the old notion of the sovereign right to control its boundaries and to exclude whatever aliens it wants to exclude, remains to be seen.

19. See 1A. C. Gordon and H. Rosenfeld, *Immigration Law and Procedure* (New York: Matthew Bender, 1984), Sec. 5.5–5.13 (1982).

20. By "eventual" I mean post-*Fong*.

21. For a good discussion of the dialogue between the Court and the other two branches of government with regard to the deportation of subversives see T. Alexander Aleinikoff and David Martin, *Immigration: Process and Policy* (St. Paul: West Publishing Co., 1985), chapter 5.

22. Perhaps the leading case before *Fleuti* was *Volpe v. Smith*, 289 U.S. 422 (1933). In this case the resident alien had lived in the United States continuously for twenty-two years, but then made the grave mistake of visiting Cuba. When Volpe attempted to come back to this country he was excluded, the Court agreeing with the INS that this was an "entry." The practical significance of the reentry doctrine in cases like *Volpe* is that the government is allowed to exclude "undesirable" resident aliens after statutory limits to deport have passed. For example, in this case nineteen years after his entry into the United States Volpe was convicted of counterfeiting obligations of the United States. The Court stated that this act was one which was "plainly a crime involving moral turpitude." (p. 422.)

23. INA § 101 (a)(13), 8 U.S.C. § 1101 (a)(13) defines an "entry" as "any coming of an alien into the United States, from a foreign port or place or from an outlying possession, whether voluntarily or otherwise, except that an alien having a lawful permanent residence in the United

States shall not be regarded as making an entry into the United States for the purposes of the immigration laws if the alien proves to the satisfaction of the Attorney General that his departure to a foreign port or place or to an outlying possession was not intended or reasonably to be expected by him or his presence in a foreign port or place or in an outlying possession was not voluntary...."

24. 426 U.S. 67 (1976).

25. 459 U.S. 21 (1982).

26. 459 U.S. at 32.

27. For a good discussion of this see Note, "Immigration Policy and the Rights of Aliens," *Harvard Law Review* 96 (1983): 1286–1465; see also Peter Mutharika, *The Alien Under American Law* (New York: Ocean Pub., 1981).

28. *Truax v. Rauch*, 239 U.S. 33 (1915).

29. 403 U.S. 365 (1971).

30. 435 U.S. 291 (1978).

31. 441 U.S. 68 (1979).

32. 454 U.S. 432 (1982).

33. One of the ironies here is that at the same time that one branch of the national government was expressing concern for the political community of the individual states, another branch was disregarding such considerations in the area of refugee resettlement. Southeast Asian refugees were unceremoniously and unexpectedly "dumped" on a large number of communities throughout the country. See generally U.S. Cong., House, Hearings before the Subcommittee on Immigration, Refugees, and International Law of the Committee on the Judiciary, *Refugee Act of 1980 Amendment*, 97th Cong., 1st sess. Mar. 24, 1981.

34. 426 U.S. 67 (1976).

35. 426 U.S. 88 (1976).

36. 426 U.S. at 102 (cites omitted).

37. See Gerald Rosberg, "Aliens and Equal Protection: Why Not the Right to Vote?" *University of Michigan Law Review* 77 (1977): 1092–1136.

38. 457 U.S. 202 (1982).

39. 457 U.S. at 223.

40. See Michael Piore's classic work *Birds of Passage: Migrant Labor and Industrial Society* (New York: Cambridge University Press, 1980); see also Susan Forbes, "The Half Open Door: Illegal Migration to the United States," *U.S. Immigration Policy and the National Interest, Staff Report of the Select Commission on Immigration and Refugee Policy*, 457.

Part II
Developing a New Alien Admission System

Chapter 6
Individual Obligations

The object of this chapter is to determine whether individuals should have some moral responsibility for the actions of their government, or to phrase it another way, whether individuals should have moral responsibilities in the international arena. I argue that despite free rider problems, individual citizens do have such moral obligations, although the burden of carrying out these obligations will, at times, fall on the national government itself. In the latter part of this chapter I address the unique problems caused by alien admissions.

Although it is generally assumed that individuals should act morally, philosophers have not been able to effectively fashion an argument that will convince any and all skeptics.[1] I work under the assumption that individuals should act morally. I also assume that individuals generally want to act morally. The question I address is whether these common assumptions on the domestic level should also apply to the international realm as well. Because my discussion views citizen responsibility in a rather nontraditional manner, I also need to point out that I am quite willing to work within the structure of the current nation-state system.

My position is that citizens of a state have some moral responsibility for the actions of their government. Henry Shue has argued that a state acts as agent for its citizens:

> Apart from duties to avoid depriving, which are owed to every person, relatively few duties are borne by the national government of any nation in its own right toward persons living in other nations, as opposed to being performed by the government acting as agent for some of, or all, its own constituents.[2]

I think this is an apt and desirable description and I shall defend this position.

It needs to be pointed out that I am not arguing that those in policy positions are without particular moral obligations.[3] In fact, I think it could be argued quite effectively that those in policy positions will have a greater responsibility to act because of the unique position that they are in. However, the obligations of policymakers should not obscure or necessarily override the obligations that citizens themselves might have. Nonetheless, the notion of citizen responsibility has been a minority position. James Fishkin defends the dominant view: "It is characteristically liberal assumptions that require us, too easily, as individuals to assume the full burdens of large-scale, public problems—those that might better be left to collectivities, nation-states, and other large institutions."[4]

Contrary to Fishkin's assertions, it is not apparent that a great number of political philosophers do in fact espouse the position that individuals should tackle large-scale public problems. It is even less evident that individuals are actively attempting to assume such burdens. The massive number of donations by private individuals to Ethiopian relief, however, might prove the latter assertion wrong. At the same time, it might also prove wrong those who argue that there is very little individuals themselves can do.

Stanley Hoffman has recently looked at the role of morality in international relations and I think his "realpolitik" conception of the issue shows why it is so difficult to promote moral concerns in this area generally, particularly the notion of citizens having moral obligations.[5] Hoffman divides moral obligations into three separate categories: (1) the moral obligations of policymakers, (2) the moral obligations of those who have to carry out the directives of policymakers, and (3) the moral obligations of what he terms " the rest of us."

Although Hoffman purports to talk about the moral duties of all three groups, essentially he ignores the moral obligations of the second category, and he offers a very limited view of the moral responsibilities of "the rest of us." Added to this, Hoffman accepts the notion that nations pay a severe price for acting morally in the international realm to begin with.[6] What this ignores, of course, is that acting morally will often entail some cost. Simply stated, these costs make moral actions more difficult, but not any less compelling.

The portion of Hoffman's argument that I want to focus on is his depiction of the role to be played by citizens in a Western democracy. Citizens, he argues, are to throw the rascals out of office through the power of the franchise. In addition, Hoffman believes that citizens can lobby their elected representatives. Although Hoffman gives an accurate depiction of the democratic process in a society such as ours (actually the ideal), it is noteworthy that he gives little substance to his discussion of individual moral objectives. In other words, Hoffman asserts that "the rest of us" will have moral obligations as citizens, yet it is never clear what those obligations would entail beyond voting rascals out of office. It is never even clear what makes a politician a rascal. Because Hoffman promotes the idea that national leaders are to act as "trustees" for that society, one can only presume that a rascal is one who does not promote the best interest of the members of that society. In sum, Hoffman purports to speak about the obligations of citizens, but he offers a very limited vision. The moral obligations of citizens are either no different from those of policymakers, or else they are subsumed by the interests of policymakers.

One explanation for this limited view of citizen responsibility is that Hoffman's views are based on an "ought implies can" premise, and he sees citizens being able to accomplish very little: "How much can citizens actually accomplish? At a minimum, they can vote.... They can, by their pressures on their representatives or by their own efforts, affect at least some things. ..."[7] Again, Hoffman is not clear what it is that citizens should hope to accomplish, but I will not belabor this criticism.

This notion that there is very little that individuals themselves can do is commonly accepted, and it seems to be the most prevalent argument against individual responsibility in the international realm. Susan James argues that not only is there little that individuals can do to relieve harm, but individuals themselves are not in a position to cause much harm either:

> a concern with the responsibilities of groups might be regarded as a merit, rather than a defect, of an argument which aims to reveal the extent of our obligations to relieve and prevent harm, for much of the harm which afflicts people is both caused by groups and of a kind which can most readily be relieved by them. Single individuals often cannot do a great deal to prevent famine and disease, and they are relatively powerless to wreak these ills on others. But governments, hospitals, and corporations can obviously make great changes in the world.[8]

Because of its theoretical importance, this capacity argument needs close examination. The first response to this position is the most obvious: individuals do make a difference. Again I point to the outpouring of aid for Ethiopian relief from private U.S. citizens. Related to this, there is no reason why individuals have to accomplish a great deal. Fishkin's earlier comment about assuming the "full burdens of large-scale, public problems," and James's statement that individuals "cannot do a great deal" are based on a faulty premise. Moral obligations should not be based on the amount that individuals can accomplish. To employ a variant of Singer's example, if there are fifteen children drowning, but a passerby only has the energy to save one, this fact should not remove the obligation to save this one child. What is more accurate is that we should not inform the exhausted lifesaver: you had a moral obligation to save all fifteen children. Fishkin and James might possibly be speaking of a moral overload problem, but their limitations on moral obligations seem to be premised on the idea that because individuals could not accomplish a whole lot they therefore should not have any moral obligations for large-scale, public problems.

Another response to the dominant position is that even if individuals themselves do not have the ability to make a difference, they can quite easily join some interest group which can make a difference. This is to say that individuals will often have the capacity to have the "can." There will be free rider problems, but the free rider problem should not imply "can't," nor should such problems imply that moral obligations do not exist. Instead, the free rider problems arise out of self-interested behavior which cannot be equated with moral behavior. The issue is whether the principle that "ought implies can" should limit the moral obligations that individual citizens have in the international arena. My point is that the "can" is not as much of a problem as it has been portrayed. Finally, even if we assume that individuals (or groups) can accomplish very little, there is no reason why governments are precluded from carrying out the moral obligations of their citizens. In fact, this is a function that governments ought to perform.

The prevalent view sees governments acting in the purported best interests of society. This is the trustee argument alluded to earlier. Brian Barry argues that this position has often been used to ignore moral concerns, the view apparently being that the best interests of a society do not necessarily include a moral interest.[9] My point is that nations can act as trustees. However, there is no logical reason why the moral component should be removed when a nation acts as a trustee for its citizens.

Thus far I have concentrated on the rationales often given for removing moral responsibility from individual citizens in the international realm. My point is that on closer examination these are not compelling arguments. However, providing a positive response to the question of why individuals have moral responsibilities in the international realm is more difficult. The best answer seems to be that individuals should act morally because in doing so they exercise their own autonomy, and at the same time they respect the autonomy of other individuals. As I stated earlier, acting morally does not entail doing that which is politically expedient, or avoiding what is inconvenient or difficult. It is only when individuals recognize and go beyond their immediate self-interest that they act as autonomous beings; only in doing so can other individuals be treated as autonomous beings as well. Although individuals might share in a communal life with other "members," this should not preclude individuals from respecting the autonomy of other individuals beyond national borders. That is, even if one presumed the existence of a tightly knit community, it does not follow from this that "strangers" should not be treated as autonomous individuals. There is no zero-sum game between respecting the autonomy of other members and those who are not members. I conclude, then, that individuals do in fact have moral obligations in the international realm, and that the nation of which they are members should act as their agent in carrying out these obligations. In later chapters I refer to particular nations having certain duties, but this is done for convenience, and it is not meant to detract from obligations that citizens will have.

CONCLUSION

I have argued in this chapter that individual citizens have moral obligations in the international realm. How does this translate into an alien admission policy? Although citizens have obligations, this does not mean that individual citizens should employ their own alien admission system. In fact, just the opposite rule should be followed.[10] Unlike private relief activities, to use that example, a citizen following his or her own alien admission system will pursue activities that will have serious consequences (many negative) on the community itself. In essence, admitting strangers to a community is qualitatively different from providing economic aid, even if the purpose of both is to provide aid to those in serious need. Alien admission policy, then, is primarily the concern of the larger political community. The one exception that should be made, however, would be instances where a nation has caused great harm to individuals in other lands, or it has put itself in a position where it is likely that great harm will occur from its actions, *and* the government of that nation refuses to meet any obligations to those affected individuals. In those instances, and only those instances, individual citizens have a duty to provide aid, notwithstanding the fact that this goes against government policy.

NOTES

1. For example, Charles Fried has attempted to address this issue in this manner: "And so to the question why should we be moral, I would answer that no obligation to be moral can be adduced. One either is or is not moral, with all the ensuing consequences for the individual and his relations.... If one asks 'why should I be moral,' the answer is 'you are under no obligation to be moral, but if you are moral, these and these are your obligations.' " *An Anatomy of Values: Problems of Personal and Social Choice* (Cambridge: Harvard University Press, 1970), 60.
2. Henry Shue, *Basic Rights: Subsistence, Affluence, and U.S. Foreign Policy* (Princeton: Princeton University Press, 1980), 150.
3. See Thomas Nagel, "Ruthlessness in Public Life," in Stuart Hampshire, ed., *Public and Private Morality* (New York: Cambridge University Press, 1978).
4. James Fishkin, *The Limits of Obligation* (New Haven: Yale University Press, 1982), 9.
5. Stanley Hoffman, *Duties Beyond Borders: On the Limits and Possibilities of Ethical International Politics* (Syracuse: Syracuse University Press, 1981).
6. Hoffman writes: "What are the consequences of these limits on moral choice? The most evident could be called the moral inferiority of international politics. This is a domain in which, much more than in domestic politics, one pays a penalty for behaving decently." *Duties Beyond Borders*, 23.
7. Ibid., 229.
8. Susan James, "The Duty to Relieve Suffering," *Ethics* 93 (1982): 19.
9. Brian Barry, *Rich Countries and Poor Countries* (unpublished manuscript, quoted with permission of the author), chapter 1.
10. Walzer takes a similar position: "Are citizens bound to take in strangers? Let us assume that they have no formal obligations; they are bound by nothing more stringent than the principle of mutual aid or Good Samaritanism. The principle must be applied, however, not to individuals directly but to the citizens as a group, for immigration is a matter of political decision. Individuals participate in the decision-making, if the state is democratic, but they decide not for themselves, but for the community generally." Michael Walzer, "The Distribution of Membership," in Peter Brown and Henry Shue, eds., *Boundaries: National Autonomy and Its Limits* (Totowa, N.J.: Rowman and Littlefield, 1981), 16.

Chapter 7
The Harm Principle

THE PRINCIPLE ITSELF

The Harm Principle (HP) has two parts to it. The first is that individuals have a duty not to harm others. The second part states that those who have caused harm have a special duty of restitution to the victims of this harm. The HP seeks to protect the autonomy of the individual. Other individuals should not violate this autonomy by causing harm to another individual. When this autonomy has been violated the individual who has violated another person's autonomy should make restitution.

Assume there are three individuals, X, Y, and Z who have all been seriously wounded. X was wounded by A and Y was wounded by B. Z was harmed by a natural disaster. Under the first part of the HP, A should not have harmed X (assuming no possible justification, such as self-defense). The second part of the HP states that because A has harmed X she now has an affirmative duty to aid X. Because A has not harmed Y or Z she does not have a duty to aid either Y or Z under the HP. This, however, does not fully answer all of the duties that A might have. In the next chapter I will turn to a possible duty that A might have to Y and Z under the Basic Rights Principle (BRP).

The notion of not harming others is such an intuitive concept that it nearly defies justification. One might attempt to ground this idea on something as basic as the golden rule, but I do not think this offers a sufficient explanation. A better explanation is that one overriding moral principle is to protect the autonomy of the individual, and that autonomy is not protected when individuals are harmed by others. The notion of helping those we have harmed finds widespread support in the philosophical literature. For example, Joel Feinberg writes: "When your loss is 'my fault,' that is when it was caused by my negligence, recklessness, impulsiveness, carelessness, dishonesty, malevolence, or the like, then I have a duty to you to repair the harm or otherwise make good the loss."[1] David Miller takes a similar position:

> Rights to compensation arise when one person deliberately or negligently harms another, or injures his interest in some way. If I knock you over in the street, you have a right that I help you to your feet again. If I damage your house, you have a right that I make good the loss.[2]

H. L. A. Hart's distinction between general and special rights is useful to a discussion of the HP.[3] There is a general right not to be harmed by others because this violates the autonomy of the individual. All individuals have a general duty not to be harm others, although some—those who have put themselves in a position where they might cause serious harm to others— have a stronger duty not to harm. I discussed this higher duty not to harm in Chapter 3 and I will return to it throughout this chapter. After an individual has been harmed, she has a special right to aid from the person who has caused the harm. Likewise, the individual who has caused the harm has a special duty to aid the injured party. The act of harm, by itself, creates this special duty and this special right. It is the existence of these special rights and duties that makes the HP a stronger obligation than the BRP, where such special rights and duties do not exist. Because the HP seeks to hold individuals responsible for acts of harm that they have performed, it only applies to acts of commission and not to acts of omission. The latter would fall under the aegis of the BRP. The HP is a very concerted effort to hold individuals responsible for the harm that they have caused. I not only hope to be able to show the necessity of this as an important first step in meeting the needs of others, but I will also show situations where the HP should apply.

Not all philosophers agree that finding the cause of harm is so imperative. T. D. Campbell argues that aid should be based on a principle of negative utilitarianism where the object of human endeavor would be to relieve suffering where it is the greatest. Campbell continues, "We would regard it as inhuman to make relief for refugees dependent on proof of their innocence, or the assistance of wounded persons or malformed children dependent on who, if anybody, was responsible for the occurrence of the injury or malfunction."[4]

If Campbell is arguing that the cause of need is generally irrelevant than I think he is mistaken. Only by understanding who is responsible for the need of others can we begin to place certain moral obligations on definite individuals for specific actions. Walzer thinks that the "members-strangers" dichotomy is the proper distinction to make in order to limit moral obligations and to make them meaningful. However, Walzer is also cognizant that there might be some moral obligations to those outside our national borders, particularly to those we have harmed. Likewise, Henry Shue suggests that it is important to single out those who have caused harm—for example, the Dutch for their actions in Java.

If Campbell is saying, instead, that an inordinate concern with the cause of the need of others ultimately makes for little or no aid, then I think he is on much firmer ground. Under the theory presented here, however, causing or not causing serious harm or need is only the first step in analysis, albeit an important one. Even if an individual has not caused a particular harm, she might have some moral obligation under the BRP to those in serious need. It is essential to note, however, that the duty under the BRP is not a special duty, nor is this duty as far-ranging as the duty under the HP.

In addition to a wide acceptance in the philosophical literature, there is a solid foundation for both provisions of the HP in the law, both domestic law and international law. For example, tort law in this country is largely premised on the idea that individuals should not harm others, and that restitution is obligated when harm has occurred. This is civil law in its rawest, simplest, and most essential form. There has even been a recent move in the field of criminal law to treat crimes as violations against individuals, rather than, or in addition to, being transgressions against the state.[5]

The tort law analogy is further strengthened when we look at how the actions of those who have been harmed might, under some circumstances, lessen or even eliminate the responsibility of those perpetrating harm. In tort law the assumption of risk doctrine limits the liability of an individual causing harm when others have freely chosen to accept risk.[6] Likewise, under the HP those who accept certain risks generally should not be able to hold responsible those who ultimately cause harm. The most common scenario is when one nation invites another nation, or entities of this other nation (such as multinational corporations), to perform rather routine activities in the first nation, such as business activities. In Part I the notion of respecting communal autonomy was repeatedly stressed. One way to achieve this would be to follow this general rule: when one nation invites another nation to do business in that country it is "as if" the inviting nation were merely performing such activities itself. If harm thereby occurs, the act of inviting outsiders to perform such actions will be an important consideration in determining if the HP should be invoked. Again, this general rule is analogous to the assumption of risk principle in American tort law.

This general rule, however, should only go so far. The rationale for the rule, as I stated before, is to protect the autonomy of other societies. The presumption (a rebuttable one) is that a ruling regime knows what is best for that particular society, and that outside nations should not meddle in such affairs of other countries. Where we should not remove responsibility from a nation that has been invited to perform certain actions in another society would be: (1) where there is great harm or the potential for great harm, but where it appears that no action will be taken to prevent such harm, (2) where the host country is not able to exercise its autonomy because it possesses little bargaining power vis-à-vis outside actors, and (3) where the inviting nation would be considered unjust by the standards of international law and international morality.

I do not mean to portray these criteria as somehow mutually exclusive, nor should the list be seen as exhausting all possible means of protecting the autonomy of individuals in other countries under such special circumstances. These exceptions to the general rule that an inviting nation assumes all or most risks when it invites another nation to do business are grounded on the idea that under certain circumstances a nation will not, or cannot, protect its sovereign autonomy or the autonomy of its citizens. The exceptions seek to protect against exploitable situations.

As a final point on this particular matter, the general rule under discussion assumes a routine state of affairs between two nations. When we are speaking of special types of circumstances this general rule should not apply. War is a good example of this. Although nation A might invite nation B to participate in a war in A, this does not remove the special responsibility that the government of B and the soldiers of B would have not to harm noncombatants. The reason for this is that in this situation B presumably has much more control, or the ability to have control, over whether citizens of A have their basic rights met. In addition, serious harm is also much more likely in war situations than where two nations are merely transacting business.

Although the HP has certain tort law analogies, it is important to note that the HP is much more limited in its scope than tort law is. While tort law seeks to protect the autonomy of the individual from virtually all types of invasion,[7] the HP, on the other hand, only seeks to protect against, and make restitution for, serious harms to individuals. The HP is not invoked by technical violations of an individual's autonomy, or even by harms that are less than serious. A similar and I think very useful approach has been taken by Henry Shue in his seminal work "Exporting Hazards." Although Shue's inquiry is not directly on point—he is concerned with the amount of information foreign workers should have about job safety—his reasoning is quite applicable to the current discussion. Shue talks about protecting "life, limb, and vitality" and that is the present concern also.

This "life, limb, and vitality" standard is open to criticism from both sides. Some might think that it is not restrictive enough. For instance, Singer might be read to mean that only those who are in mortal danger have valid claims for immediate aid. The criticism from the other side might be that individual autonomy is violated in a number of ways aside from instances of serious harm.

To begin with the first line of criticism, death is too demanding a standard. Aside from its finality, there is little to distinguish between death and the kinds of harms the HP seeks to protect against. That is, there is little to differentiate between a life filled with severe pain and suffering and the loss of that life. If we change Singer's example so that a young child is being tortured nearby, our intuitive reaction would differ little from the example of the drowning child. To respond to the criticism from the other side, it is important to consider that the purpose of the present effort is not to create an international tort system. The world may evolve to that, but it certainly has not done so yet. In seeking to protect against serious harms, I am arguing that there are degrees of violations against individual autonomy, and the HP seeks to protect against the most serious ones. To use a domestic example, most people would feel something was quite amiss if our law enforcement agencies devoted most of their resources to prevent simple assaults while murder and rape was rampant.

To return to the example used earlier, if A had only wounded X slightly, and if Z and Y were in serious need, then A's duty would be to Y and Z and not X (assuming that A's duty under the Basic Rights Principle extended this far, which I will address in the next chapter). The harder case is where X is seriously wounded by A but X's condition is not quite as grave as that of Y and Z. Where would A's duty lie? Obviously these are difficult choices to make. In principle I am not against Campbell's negative utilitarian approach of giving aid to those with the greatest need. I am convinced, however, than this approach is ultimately not very workable. I maintain that an important first step in meeting the needs of individuals like X, Y, and Z is to first establish who has caused that need (if in fact anyone has, I will discuss phenomena like natural disasters in the next chapter), and to hold that person, or that nation, responsible. In this particular example, I would argue that A's strongest duty would be to X, notwithstanding the fact that X's present need is slightly less than Y and Z's. A has caused serious harm to X and this should be the determining factor.

The HP is an attempt to have nations take their duties to others quite seriously. Perhaps the clearest way to understand the very serious nature of the HP is to consider the extraordinary phenomenon that it will invoke in certain circumstances—alien admissions. The argument made here is that in order to avoid serious harm, or in order to make restitution for harm that has already occurred, a nation might have to admit "strangers" for a certain period of time. This is not to say that alien admissions will be the sole or main vehicle used to prevent individuals from being harmed or to make restitution for those who have been harmed. In fact, because of the need to protect the autonomy of receiving communities, and also because alien admissions seems to be an inefficient means of giving aid, alien admissions should generally be a means of last resort. However, the point to be made here is that alien admission should be an integral part of preventing harm, and also aiding those in need. In fact, I argue in Chapter 10 that a nation's alien admission system should first honor these moral obligations before it attempts to meet other kinds of national goals.

Before turning to international applications of the HP, I think it is useful to underline the extent of the special duty under the HP. In the next chapter I will discuss a notion of "Fair Share" that limits the duty under the BRP. There is no such limit under the HP. If a nation has not caused much harm in the world then it will have few, if any, obligations under the HP. On the other extreme, if a nation has caused a great deal of harm to individuals in the world it will have very burdensome moral obligations.

I have mentioned that there are analogies to the HP in international law. Perhaps the clearest examples of this are instances of war reparations. Nations are often forced to pay restitution to those they have harmed in the course of waging war. What weakens this analogy somewhat, I think, are the political overtones that have been synonymous with war reparations in this century. The principle itself—nations have obligations not to harm individuals in other countries and a special duty of restitution when they have caused harm—is more important than its past application.[8]

Much like the domestic examples of the HP, the notion of not harming others is rather implicit in the international arena. I would point out, however, that this principle is not as strong there as it is within the confines of a liberal society like the United States.[9] One reason for this is the "trustee" argument explored earlier. Under this dominant view, harm to individuals in other societies is seen as an unfortunate but unavoidable by-product in the pursuit of national interests. This view, combined with a decided lack of judicial and administrative machinery on both the international and domestic scenes,[10] weakens the present-day application of the HP. This is not to say that efforts to hold nations responsible for all harm that they have caused should not be made. However, the first and most important task is to protect against instances of serious harm. This is what the HP seeks to achieve.

GENERAL EXAMPLES OF THE PRINCIPLE

In this section I turn my attention to instances where individuals get "harmed" by other countries, or individuals or corporations from other countries. I look at war situations, other instances where subsistence rights are threatened, and the support of unjust regimes. These three general phenomena are not meant to be an exhaustive list of ways that individuals get harmed. However, each of these phenomena occurs quite frequently, while at the same time "harm" is usually not automatically associated with them. My intent is to explain when and why the HP should apply.

War

One way in which individuals get harmed, sometimes fatally, is through the waging of war. War, almost by definition, means destruction, disease, and death or maiming. My position is that when one nation wages war in another society this intervening nation should be guided by the HP. That is, there is a duty not to harm others, and a special duty to aid those who have been harmed. I am not suggesting that the HP applies equally to every person in situations where war is waged. Some individuals have assumed the risks of war, others have not.[11] Michael Walzer has given this very solid account for the philosophical distinction that is drawn between combatants and noncombatants.

When we say, war is hell, it is the victims of the fighting that we have in mind. In fact, then, war is the very opposite of hell in the theological sense, and is hellish only when the opposition is strict. For in hell, presumably, only those people suffer who deserve to suffer, who have chosen activities for which punishment is the appropriate divine response, knowing that this is so. But the greater number by far of those who suffer in war have made no comparable choice.[12]

I want to build from this distinction. I propose not only that noncombatants be protected, but I claim that in some instances the only means of doing this is by the admission of noncombatants to the intervening nation or some other country.[13]

Some might respond to my argument that war invokes the HP by arguing that a nation only participates in a war to avoid some greater harm. This argument runs along these lines: although war will bring some harm, our involvement has prevented (or will prevent) some greater harm from occurring. As a result, this argument continues, the HP is not applicable because intervention has averted some greater harm. There is overwhelming evidence available to suggest that war is very often waged merely to pursue national goals, and that little consideration is given to the harm to civilians that war might bring.[14] Even if we were to assume, for the purposes of discussion, that a particular war did in fact avoid some greater harm to another society, this would still not make the HP inapplicable. The HP states that noncombatants have a basic right not to be harmed, and that strong efforts should be made to protect the autonomy of individuals who have not accepted the risks attendant with war. This is not to argue that the number of noncombatant lives that would be lost is not an important consideration. Obviously it should be. However, the importance of this consideration lies in the decision whether to participate in a war in the first place. It should not be used to claim that in waging war no harm has occurred because more lives have been saved (or will be saved) than would have occurred without the war.

My position might be read to say that an intervening nation might have some duty to enemy noncombatants under the HP, perhaps a duty to grant admission to these noncombatants. I will not disagree with this argument, although I will point out that in practice this seems less than likely, if for no other reason than logistics, or the wishes of the enemy noncombatants themselves. In an effort to protect noncombatants' lives, international law does not distinguish between friendly and enemy noncombatants; soldiers are not to harm either group. It will be true that there will be a stronger affinity with noncombatants who are on "our side," but this could partly be explained on the basis that public opinion, and perhaps policymakers, do not sufficiently distinguish between various sectors of "the enemy." All are summarily treated as one entity. I think this lack of distinction serves a convenient political purpose, but it should not be allowed to perpetuate itself. This example also shows how affinities can easily be mistaken for obligations. The two are not the same. Just because there is no affinity for enemy noncombatants does not mean that there are no moral obligations to protect them from harm.

In the concluding chapter I argue that our alien admission system should be set up so that priority goes to those who meet HP and BRP criteria before we seek to meet other national goals, such as reuniting families. I do not want to go into this discussion at the present time. I raise this issue now merely to address the issue of how the admission of aliens under the HP (and under the BRP although I purposely limit my discussion) would be different than the alien admission system this country has at present. Obviously the grounds for admission, and the types of individuals who would be granted admission, would be vastly different from current practice. This much should be apparent. In addition, while present day normal flow immigration practice and refugee admissions are based on a system of having aliens achieve permanent resident status and ultimately citizenship in this country, admission under the HP would not have this as its premise. Instead, the HP seeks to prevent serious harm before it occurs, and to make restitution for harm caused. This does not necessarily entail permanent residence in the country of resettlement.

Consider this example: country O intervenes in a war in nation P. M is a noncombatant of P. Country O admits M in order to provide her safety from this war. When the war ends M's continued residence in O is no longer warranted. O still has a duty not to harm M, but this duty does not have to be performed with M living in O. In fact, because the admission of aliens might serve to disrupt the community of O, or subcommunities in O, such practices are generally discouraged. O might also have a duty of restitution to a citizen like M—perhaps the agricultural land in P has been made fallow by the war. Again, however, this does not dictate M's continued residence in O. Restitution can be made in other ways.

The difficulty arises when individuals have stayed for a considerable period of time in another country and they have developed certain life plans in that country that might have little meaning in the original homeland. A good example of this might be if the United States attempted to repatriate some of the Cubans and Vietnamese who have already lived in the United States for a long period of time. Obviously such situations will present difficult public policy choices. Walzer tries to make the problem easier by positing that the Vietnamese had effectively become Americans, but this is not true. The general rule, as harsh as it might seem, is that after the threat of harm has ceased, repatriation, in the situation outlined above, should be the policy pursued. This is not to say that somehow these individuals would not be either inconvenienced or even "harmed" under a much looser definition of that term than is being used here. It is quite likely that life plans contingent upon continued residence in this country have been made. However, unless an individual who is to be repatriated would suffer serious harm upon being returned, repatriation is warranted.

Some discussion is needed of where noncombatants fleeing harm under a war situation should be resettled. If noncombatants can in fact be provided safety within the nation where war is being waged, then this policy should be pursued. Individuals would not have to be uprooted from their homeland, nor would other societies be disrupted by having to receive such strangers.

In addition, Charles Keely has persuasively argued that refugee resettlement is a very inefficient means of providing assistance to those in serious need.[15] Keely's basic argument is that economic assistance will go much further than providing aid through the cumbersome and expensive method of alien admissions. In war situations (although this applies to other ways of harming others as well), the admission of noncombatants should not be the first policy employed in an effort to protect them or to aid them.

It needs to be stressed, more than once I suppose, that the duties under the HP need to be taken quite seriously. If in fact the safety of noncombatants in the homeland during a war is quite doubtful, resettlement in other countries is morally dictated. Which countries? It is important to remember the distinction between special and general duties and who has what duty. Take the example of an ongoing war. A nation that is participating in a war in another country will have a special duty to protect noncombatants in this country. The reason for this is that by participating in a war this intervening nation has placed itself in a position where it might cause great harm. Nations that are not involved in fighting such a war will only have a general duty to protect or to aid these same noncombatants. As a result, intervening nations have stronger moral obligations than nonintervening nations.

This is not to say, however, that resettlement is only warranted in intervening nations and not in nations that have not intervened. For one thing, the latter group might have some duty to admit these noncombatants under the BRP. Beyond this, it might also be possible for nations that have special duties to meet these moral responsibilities through resettlement in third countries. For example, an intervening nation with a special duty to noncombatants might make an agreement with another nation (presumably a nation that is much closer to the fighting) so that resettlement occurs in this other place. What should be avoided, however, are instances where a nation with a special duty to aid or protect ignores this special duty and it leaves the burdensome task of aiding those in serious need to countries with much weaker moral obligations.

Although international law does seek to protect noncombatants in war settings, it generally does not do so through admission to other countries. This is one way in which the HP differs noticeably from current international law. The definition of a refugee under international law is one who:

owing to [a] well founded fear of being persecuted for reasons of race, religion, nationality, membership of a particular social group or political opinion, is outside the country of his nationality and is unable or, owing to such fear, is unwilling to avail himself of the protection of that nationality and being outside the country of his former habitual residence as a result of such events, is unable or, owing to such fear, is unwilling to return to it.[16]

This is to say that individuals who are persecuted or have a well founded fear of persecution based on race, religion, nationality, or membership in a particular social group may achieve refugee status under current international law, but not individuals who merely fear death from war. The rationale employed is much like that in Brecht's "Mother Courage." That is, these unfortunates are simply the victims of war, but no one is taking special pains to inflict injury on them.

David Martin has remarked on this exception: "The theory behind this technical limitation on the refugee category is apparently that the bombs will cease falling, the floods will recede, but persecution is implacable."[17] Despite this rather tongue-in-cheek rationale, Martin, surprisingly enough, defends this practice: "It distinguishes those uprooted persons who are more likely to be able to pick up the pieces of their lives again in the place where they originated, and who therefore have less need of resettlement in a distant land."[18]

The rationale for excluding individuals fleeing wars makes little sense theoretically.[19] It might well be an effort to place a limit on the number of people who could justifiably leave a country during a war, but the definition is a rather blunt instrument. Martin's rationale for excluding certain groups points to some valid rationales. However, there is no reason why any or all victims of wars would be any better able to "pick up the pieces" than would the victims of the listed means of persecution. In fact, one could look at a phenomenon like the sudden transformation in Argentina under the Alfonsin regime and argue that it is much easier and quicker to transform an unjust regime into a just one than it would be to transform a war-torn society into one that was not afflicted by all of the horrors brought on by war. Finally, Martin's explanation generally speaks to situations after a war, thus the language about picking up the pieces. What this does not address is the question of protecting the basic rights of noncombatants during a war. Picking up the pieces is not the primary aim of noncombatants at that time, survival is.

Other Causes of Harm

There are many other ways besides war in which individuals get harmed by other nations. Because of the inabilities of the judicial and administrative machineries in many other countries to control these types of situations (in addition to ineffective international tribunals), as well as the common acceptance of the "trustee" argument, it is not as natural to speak of "harm" in the international realm as it is in the domestic. Despite this, nations, and entities of other nations, can cause great harm in other societies.

Another difference between the harms presently under discussion and the war example is that it is much more natural to speak of alien admissions in the context of the latter rather than the former (although efforts at resettlement seem to occur *after* the war). To my knowledge, no one has suggested granting admission to the victims of the Union Carbide chemical leak disaster in Bhopal, India, where 200,000 individuals were injured in addition to the 2,000 who died. The HP does have an applicability beyond the question of alien admissions. These other applications, however, are beyond the scope of this present work. I would argue, nonetheless, that the acceptance of the HP is quite important in its own right, beyond its use in framing an alien admissions system. In addition, I would also argue that alien admissions might have much more applicability to the kinds of situations under discussion than most people would realize.[20] I recognize, however, that unlike war and persecution, alien admission matters will often be a secondary consideration to the kinds of situations I will address in this section. For this reason I will purposely limit my discussion.

I will not say much about one nation causing harm to individuals in other societies outside of war situations. Such examples exist. I employ several examples in Chapter 9 to explore such issues. A more pressing matter involves the question of holding multinational corporations responsible for great harms that they might cause in other lands. Henry Shue has written about the need for multinational corporations to impose control on their activities in other countries.

> the government of a poor country that actually needs this kind of foreign investment—one may doubt whether the import of dangerous technology is often such a good thing for poor countries—may have no leverage against a firm that is determined to retain the less safe but cheaper technology. If "ought presupposes can," it cannot be the governments of capital-poor and technology-poor nations that ought to bring the firms with surplus capital and multiple technologies to heel. The firms themselves ought to stop inflicting harm.[21]

Although business firms will in fact need to hold themselves in check when they are faced with exploitable situations, I believe there should also be some duty on the part of the home government to control the actions of its corporations. If it can be shown that a nation knows that one of its corporations is seriously harming, or about to harm, individuals in other lands, and if it appears as if no party will prevent this from occurring, the home nation of the multinational has a responsibility to prevent this serious harm. The rationale behind this standard of care is that: (1) individuals have a basic right not to be harmed, (2) multinational corporations are capable of pursuing activities that might bring great harm, (3) some MNCs are more powerful, and have much stronger bargaining power, than the nations that are inviting them in to do business,[22] and (4) a home government might be in a better position than host nations to prevent one of its corporations from harming individuals in other societies.[23] To use a well-known example, if Nestle had been an American corporation, I think there would have been some duty on the part of the U.S. government to prevent Nestle's actions in third world countries when it was apparent that the corporation's activities were having disastrous effects.

Supporting Unjust Regimes

The last general example I will discuss is where one nation supports a regime in another country that is unjust. This might happen in a variety of ways but two common ways would be (1) where nation A works toward the overthrow of a just regime in country B and an unjust regime comes to power in B, and/or (2) where nation A works toward keeping an unjust regime in B in power, although it did not work toward its establishment in the first place. I am assuming, based on my discussion in Part I, that communities are important to individuals, and that just communities are more desirable than unjust ones. Recall Rawls's statement that there is no duty to an unjust regime. Finally, the position being taken here is that where one nation helps to establish or maintain an unjust regime in another country, this outside nation thereby causes harm to those who live under this unjust regime. Douglas MacLean takes a similar position:

> Certainly where we are responsible for having brought repressive regimes to power, we share complicity in their wrongdoings. Some of these cases, where our aid is necessary for their remaining in power, are morally equivalent to cases where we ourselves are the proximate cause of human rights violations. No doubt awareness of U.S. complicity in such cases is one of the principal explanations for the current popularity of the human rights movement.[24]

I am not assuming that philosophers have agreed on what is or is not a just or legitimate regime. In fact, philosophers seem quite at odds on the initial question whether foreigners can legitimately make such determinations. Although my discussion focuses on other matters, I think it is essential to pursue this question of what is a just or legitimate regime. I will define a legitimate regime simply as a regime that the majority in a particular society want to see in power, for whatever reason. Although this definition might seem to have a Western democratic bias, there are no assurances that a majority of individuals in a society would choose this kind of government. In that respect it is neutral with respect to the system ultimately chosen. Walzer has stressed that societies should have the ability to choose their own form of government and governors, and to a large extent I think he is correct. I would argue, however, that a legitimate regime is not necessarily a just regime. A just regime is one that works toward meeting the basic rights of its citizens. This does not say that it necessarily meets these basic rights, only that it seriously works towards meeting them.

Michael Walzer has framed the nature of the debate in terms of what actions outside nations should take when there are perceived wrongs in other societies.[25] I think the debate has been framed in extreme terms, and I think this is unnecessary and unfortunate. For one thing, the debate has largely centered around the question of when military intervention in another society would be warranted. This is a stark remedy. I would argue that the debate could just as well center around how other nations could work toward helping those who are persecuted in another society without military intervention, for example, through an alien admission system.[26] In this way we do not have the same kinds of concerns about violating the autonomy of other societies, at the same time that we attempt to meet the basic rights of others. If persecution is rampant then, but essentially *only* then, military intervention should be seriously considered. Absent this, alien admission practices would generally be a more desirable policy than military intervention. Is a country allowed some unjust practices? Walzer's theory seems to suggest this. He explains this result on the basis of allowing societies to evolve in their own way and so on. I do not think that nations should be accorded some unjust practices. If military intervention is our primary remedy, then it is understandable that we would only want nations to intervene when there was a complete lack of "fit" between government and community. If one discarded the premise of military intervention, and focused more on remedies for those who suffer persecution, it would no longer be so necessary, or desirable, to turn our heads to such practices.

I mentioned earlier that philosophers have been unable to agree on whether foreigners would be in a position to determine whether another regime was just or not. Again, there are very real fears of Western liberal biases or paternalism in such determinations. The concern is that if other societies are not "like us" they will therefore be judged unjust. This should not be the criteria employed. Rather than not attempting such determinations, which is implicit in Walzer's approach, I think that the best we can hope to do is to take special precautions to ensure that in attempting to pass judgment on the justness of other regimes we would be aware of these biases and attempt to overcome them. One means of doing this would be to (1) publicly espouse the standards that are being applied, (2) apply the criteria consistently across countries, and (3) respect any and all criticism of these standards that are made by other countries or by international forums.

I should point out, however, that often it might not be necessary to make broad judgments about the complete justness or the complete unjustness of a particular regime. Instead, other nations might look to certain unjust practices, and attempt to halt those, at the same time that efforts are made to offer assistance to those who suffer from these unjust practices. What must be avoided is a paralysis in providing aid to those who are harmed while nations are endlessly debating whether certain regimes are just or not, and if they are not, whether military intervention is warranted. That is, nations should not lose sight of why they are concerned with such questions in the first place.[27]

The HP states that a nation that has worked towards establishing or maintaining an unjust regime in another country therefore has harmed this nation. Moreover, the intervening nation is implicated in the unjust practices of this regime as a result of this support. This, however, does not answer the very difficult question of what it takes to be implicated in the affairs of an unjust regime. At one extreme would be instances where nation E trains and supports guerilla forces from F, and these forces overthrow the ruling just regime in F. Moreover, perhaps E provides a great deal of military and security assistance to this new regime even when it is apparent that this new government persecutes its own people. Under these circumstances, E would clearly be implicated in the unjustness of the new regime in F. The more difficult situations arise when a nation like E provides less than this type of support. One thing we need to be mindful of is the fact that nations have a great deal of intercourse among themselves. They provide economic, social, and military assistance to one another on a regular basis. Not just any action or activity will implicate one nation in the affairs of another nation. However, when there is substantial evidence so that one nation knows, or should know, that another regime is unjust, and yet this nation continues to provide military and security assistance (or when economic assistance is used for such purposes), this will be enough to implicate the nation that persists in providing this kind of support to this unjust regime.

Although one nation might be implicated in the affairs of another, and therefore have some special responsibility to prevent harm or to aid those who have been harmed, the degree of responsibility it should bear will depend on its level of involvement with that regime. Along these same lines, it is necessary to see whether a country would be more likely to have an unjust regime in power even in the absence of outside support. That is, an intervening nation will have its moral responsibilities for its support of an unjust regime lessened if it cannot be shown that "but for" its support this other nation would have a just regime. Even in these circumstances, however, the mere fact of supporting an unjust regime will implicate an outside nation to some degree.

It is also necessary to be very clear that a nation that supports an unjust regime in another country will have varying duties to individuals living in this country depending on the level of harm suffered by them. The distinction that I will be making now is not generally made. Michael Walzer suggests that there is an ideological affinity with all of those who live under authoritarian regimes. Shue's position is that regimes that deny citizens the right to participate in the process of governing are thereby denying a basic right. This would mean that vast numbers of individuals throughout the world are being denied this basic right. This is not a very helpful way of distinguishing between the needs of individuals. Finally, Ackerman's dialogue between East and West fails to make any distinctions between various individuals in the East (or countries that comprise the East). Without this distinction we do not know if certain individuals have been singled out for persecution or not, or whether those who are admitted to the West have in fact been singled out for persecution. In addition, no effort is made to see if those admitted to the West have suffered any more than those excluded.

My point is that not all citizens living under unjust regimes will suffer the same harm from the existence of that regime. Certain individuals will be singled out for persecution, while others will "merely" suffer the daily indignities meted out by such regimes. The aid given by nations that persist in supporting unjust regimes should reflect such differences. (Although I am using a HP analysis the same reasoning would apply under an application of the BRP). That is, if a nation is unwilling to cease supporting an unjust regime, it should at least be willing to grant admission to those who are singled out for persecution in that society, assuming the threshold level of serious harm has been reached. This is less than an ideal solution, but it is better than the present state of affairs which ignores the suffering caused by regimes we support, ostensibly to avoid embarrassing them, but really to avoid embarrassing ourselves. I am somewhat dissatisfied that my proposal does not go nearly far enough in terms of a duty to the vast majority of citizens who are not singled out for persecution. Absent a cessation of support for such regimes, there is little that seems possible. It does need to be pointed out, however, that the HP and the BRP have been designed to only address issues of serious harm. Those not singled out for persecution will generally not meet this threshold.

CONCLUSION

This chapter has examined what the Harm Principle is and how and when it might apply. Rather than reiterate the arguments presented in the chapter, I will state what I am not trying to say. I am *not* arguing that nations should stop pursuing what they see as national policy goals. Instead, what I *am* saying is that in the pursuit of these goals a nation needs to be very sensitive to the human consequences of its actions in other lands. I have stressed here that a nation must take its duties to others quite seriously, and I have explained when special duties arise and what might be needed to honor them.

To conclude this chapter, Michael Teitelbaum has recently written about the mass movements of people following ill-considered foreign policy forays. His comments bear directly on what has been discussed in this chapter.

Foreign policies have frequently served (often unintentionally) to *stimulate* international migrations. In particular, foreign military or political interventions, or internal or external responses to intervention, often result in mass migrations. Foreign-policy makers rarely evaluate such effects seriously when considering intervention. Instead, they perceive the possible refugee consequences (if they consider them at all) more as a problem for "others," if the flow is to other countries, or alternatively as an obligation that the intervenor owes to local collaborators, if the intervention proves unsuccessful. Importantly, the intervening power does not necessarily see even the possible future need to admit such dependent populations as refugees as a serious cost of policy failure.[28]

NOTES

1. Joel Feinberg, *Rights, Justice, and the Bounds of Justice* (Princeton: Princeton University Press, 1980), 133.
2. David Miller, *Social Justice* (Oxford: Oxford University Press, 1976), 69.
3. H. L. A. Hart, "Are There Any Natural Rights?" *Philosophical Review* 64 (1955): 175–91.
4. T. D. Campbell, "Humanity Before Justice," *British Journal of Political Science* 4 (1974): 11.
5. See Robert Abrams, "Making a Criminal Pay Back His Victim," *New York Times*, Aug. 21, 1984, 29.
6. "In its simplest and primary sense, assumption of risk means that the plaintiff, in advance, has given his consent to relieve the defendant of an obligation of conduct toward him, and to take his chances of injury from a known risk arising from what the defendant is to do or leave undone." William Prosser, *Handbook of the Law of Torts* (St. Paul: West Publishing Co., 1971), 439.
7. Ibid., 35. "Proof of the technical invasion of the integrity of the plaintiff's person by even an entirely harmless, but offensive, contact

entitles him to vindication of his legal right by an award of nominal damages, and the establishment of the tort cause of action entitles him also to compensation for the mental disturbance inflicted upon him, such as fright or humiliation."

8. A number of very far reaching instances of restitution occurred after World War II. For a good discussion of German indemnification to the victims of Nazi terror, which still continues today in some instances, see Benjamin Ferencz, *Less Than Slaves* (Cambridge: Harvard University Press, 1979).

9. Robert Tucker has discussed certain problems in basing assistance on the notion of reparations. Tucker argues that such claims would necessarily be based on moral rather than legal claims. In addition, he argues that the moral basis would have to be today's morality and not that of many generations past where force and coercion over "backward" peoples was commonly accepted in international law. Finally, Tucker argues that respecting such claims might open a "Pandora's Box." It should be noted that Tucker's discussion of reparations is quite far-ranging (a fact that he recognizes himself) in the sense that it is looking at a coercive relationship between developed nations and developing countries quite generally. I have tried to avoid such open-ended discussions by looking for specific instances or patterns of serious harm. I have also attempted to avoid the "Pandora's Box" problem by generally limiting the applicability of the Harm Principle to instances of continuing harm. Robert Tucker, *The Inequality of Nations* (Colorado Springs: Research Committee, 1977), chapter 4.

10. For such a discussion see Richard Falk, *The Role of Domestic Courts in the International Legal Order* (Syracuse: Syracuse University Press, 1964).

11. To an extent, international law does attempt to protect noncombatants. For example, see the *Convention Relative to the Protection of Civilian Persons in War*, dated at Geneva, Aug. 12, 1949, entered into force for the United States Feb. 2, 1956, 6 U.S.T. 3516, T.I.A.S. 3365, 75 U.N.T.S. 287.

12. Michael Walzer, *Just and Unjust Wars* (New York: Basic Books, 1977), 30.

13. For further discussion of these and other issues relating to war see Elizabeth Anscombe, "War and Murder," and Richard Wasserstrom "On the Morality of War: A Preliminary Inquiry," both in Richard Wasserstrom, ed., *War and Morality* (Belmont, Calif.: Wadsworth Press, 1970); see also George Mavrodes, "Conventions and the Morality of War," *Philosophy and Public Affairs* 4 (1975); 117–31; Robert Fullinwinder, "War and Innocence," *Philosophy and Public Affairs* 5 (1975): 90–97.

14. See Hedley Bull, *The Anarchical Society: A Study of Order in World*

Politics (New York: Columbia University Press, 1977), chapter 8.

15. Charles Keely, *Global Refugee Policy: The Case for a Development-Oriented Strategy* (New York: Population Council, 1981).

16. *Geneva Convention Relating to the Status of Refugees* 19 U.S.T. 6260 T.I.A.S. 6577 (1951).

17. David Martin, "The Refugee Act of 1980: Its Past and Future," *Transnational Legal Problems of Refugees, 1982 Michigan Yearbook of International Legal Studies* (New York: Clark Boardman Company, Ltd., 1982), 101. For a excellent analysis of refugee law see Guy S. Goodwin-Gill, *The Refugee In International Law* (Oxford: Clarendon Press, 1983). For an excellent analysis of why refugee status should be extended to cover individuals whose basic rights are not being met by the home country see Andrew Shacknove, "Who Is a Refugee?" *Ethics* 95 (1985): 274–84.

18. Martin, "The Refugee Act of 1980," 101.

19. The Organization of African Unity has recognized this principle of protecting refugees from wars of aggression. See *Convention Governing the Specific Aspects of Refugee Problems in Africa*, done Sept. 10, 1964, art. I(a), U.N.T.S. no. 14691.

20. The decision by Israel to give admission to the Falasha, the Black Jews of Ethiopia, rather than send economic assistance, is noteworthy in this regard. See "Airlift to Israel Reported Taking Thousands of Jews from Ethiopia," *New York Times*, Dec. 11, 1984, 1.

21. Henry Shue, "Exporting Hazards," *Ethics* 91 (1981): 601.

22. Henry Shue, *Basic Rights: Subsistence, Affluence, and U.S. Foreign Policy* (Princeton: Princeton University Press, 1980); Ronald Muller and Richard Barnett, *Global Reach: The Power of the Multinational Corporations* (New York: Simon and Schuster, 1979).

23. For example, see Note, "Any Place But Here: A Critique of United States Hazardous Export Policy," *Brooklyn Journal of International Law* 7 (1981): 329–63.

24. Douglas MacLean, "Constraints, Goals, and Moralism in Foreign Policy," in Peter Brown and Douglas MacLean, eds., *Human Rights and U.S. Foreign Policy* (Lexington, Mass.: Lexington Books, 1979), 98.

25. See generally Walzer, *Just and Unjust Wars*, and his follow-up article, "The Moral Standing of States," *Philosophy and Public Affairs* 9 (1980): 209–29; see also the views of his four critics—Richard Wasserstrom, Charles Beitz, David Luban, and Gerald Doppelt—cited in his article.

26. For a similar argument see Jerome Slater and Terry Nardin, "Nonintervention and International Morality,"(unpublished manuscript, copy with author); see also Charles Beitz, *Political Theory and International Relations* (Princeton: Princeton University Press, 1979), 89–92.

27. For example, Michael Teitelbaum writes: "Some of the most active

advocates of Haitian migrants to the United States (especially those who are themselves Haitian exiles) appear primarily concerned with the discrediting and ultimate overthrow of the Duvalier regime rather than with the plight of the refugees themselves." "Immigration, Refugees, and Foreign Policy," *International Organization* 38 (1984): 440.

28. Ibid., 433.

Chapter 8
The Basic Rights Principle

The Basic Rights Principle (BRP), like the Harm Principle (HP), attempts to honor the basic rights of subsistence and security that individuals possess. The BRP obligates nations to play some part in meeting the basic rights of individuals in other societies even if they were not the cause of this need. I cannot hope to improve upon Henry Shue's rationale: "Why should I defend defenseless human beings? Because they are human beings and they are defenseless."[1]

Recall the example used at the beginning of the last chapter: X, Y, and Z are all seriously wounded. A has wounded X and B has wounded Y. Z is a victim of a natural disaster. A's duty to X is based on the HP. A has a special duty to aid X because she has violated X's autonomy by causing X serious harm. A has not harmed either Y or Z. Therefore, A has no special duty to aid either Y or Z. However, Y and Z possess certain basic rights as human beings. The BRP states that although A has not been responsible for the need suffered by Y and Z, A will still have some moral obligation to aid these individuals or individuals like them. This assumes that B has not met his special duty to aid Y under the HP, or that other actors have not met the needs of Y and Z. It also should be pointed out that as far as A is concerned, it does not matter that Y's need was caused by another individual while Z's need was caused by an act of nature. Both have certain basic rights as individuals that need to be met.

Exactly like the HP, the BRP seeks to remedy cases of serious need wherever and however they arise. In that respect, there is no difference between the HP and the BRP. It is also for this reason that I will not go through an analysis of how individuals are put in serious need. Except for the case of natural disasters the discussion of the previous chapter should suffice. The two principles diverge in terms of the level of obligation that each principle entails. The HP states that there is a special duty to aid all of those we have harmed (in addition to the duty not to harm in the first place). The BRP, on the other hand, does not go nearly this far. The BRP recognizes that while individuals in the world do have certain basic rights that need to be met, these needs will not be met through open-ended obligations. Recall Walzer's insightful statement: the duty to care for all will ultimately mean that no one is cared for. The BRP avoids open-ended obligations through a process known as "Fair Share."

Under the notion of Fair Share, nations would agree in advance to provide a certain amount of assistance to those in serious need that these nations were not responsible for causing. When nations have met their allotted goals they have, under my definition, met their moral obligations under the BRP, although they may not have met their stronger duties under the HP. Contrast this with Shue's notion that one's duties depended on what other nations did or did not do.

In terms of giving economic assistance to those in serious need, one figure that has often been used is 1 percent of a developed nation's Gross National Product (GNP). I will adopt this figure. That is, to meet its moral obligations under the BRP, a developed nation must give at least 1 percent (or admit a certain number of refugees, I will address this in a moment) to those in other countries in serious need. Despite its general acceptance, not every nation or political analyst has agreed to this goal. For example, Samuel Huntington has criticized the 1 percent goal in these terms:

A percentage can be a target. It is not a purpose. The aid proponents' enthusiasm for a fixed level of aid underlines a desire to escape from politics and a reluctance to develop a rationale relating aid and development to other U.S. foreign-policy goals.[2]

In defense of the proposed 1 percent figure (or something like it) it is necessary to see what it does, and why a Fair Share concept is vital. For one thing, the 1 percent figure is substantially above what developed nations are giving at present, yet it is not an onerous burden. Moreover, many nations have already agreed to the 1 percent figure as a goal. In this respect I am not suggesting anything that has not already been generally accepted. Perhaps 1 percent is not the "right" figure, but it does not exceed what many nations think is the right answer, in the abstract at least. The second purpose of the 1 percent figure is that it serves as a useful coordinating device. Nations do not have their duties expanded because other nations do not meet their own duties. Instead, nations are only morally obligated to give their agreed-upon amounts. Moreover, nations will not have the same wait-and-see incentives they have now. Obligations are much more definite.

The discussion thus far has centered around economic assistance, but that is not my primary focus. Alien admissions should also be an integral part of aid under the BRP. Again, the general rule is that if an individual could be aided by either economic assistance or alien admissions, the former is preferred over the latter. However, economic assistance can only go so far. There will be many instances when alien admission practices will need to be employed in order to meet the basic rights of others.

Like economic assistance, it should be possible for nations to work out an agreeable Fair Share formula for the admission of aliens under the BRP. Atle Grahl-Madsen, the leading scholar in the area of refugee relief, has suggested a quota system based on both the GNP per capita of a country and its population.[3] Grahl-Madsen argues that a heavier reliance should be placed on the former and his formula is: $i^{1.5}p$ where i means GNP per capita and p is population. Although Grahl-Madsen suggests using this formula (or some other related formula, he recognizes that there will be others), he also argues that nations must react to refugee flows on a case-by-case method. "Obviously, quotas or contingents must be agreed to on an ad hoc basis, as the need arises: no state is prepared to sign a blank check which would only invite abuse."[4]

I take issue with Grahl-Madsen's position on whether quotas should have some degree of permanence or not. I propose that they should. Nations should be able to meet their duties under the BRP by either giving a certain amount or percentage in economic assistance, by providing refuge to a certain number of refugees, or through some combination of these two. Moreover, nations should have the choice as to which option to follow. Grahl-Madsen's point seems to be that there is no way to determine beforehand what refugee flows will be like and therefore such efforts will necessarily be ad hoc. This is true, but only to an extent. For example, at the present time there are upwards of thirteen million refugees and displaced persons in the world. There is no apparent reason why nations could not attempt to meet these needs by arriving at some agreed quota amounts which would be applicable for as many years as it would take to resolve this state of affairs.[5]

CONCLUSION

Before turning to some examples, a few last comments need to be addressed to the HP and the BRP. I do not intend the HP and BRP to be panaceas for all of the need that exists in the world. In theory the HP and the BRP should in fact meet such needs. The HP will obligate nations to take special precautions not to harm others (so that the number of individuals in serious need should diminish considerably) and to take particular care to make restitution and provide aid when harm has been caused. The BRP obligates nations to make certain efforts to meet the basic rights of others even if they were not the cause of this need. In theory, presumably nations could agree on Fair Share amounts that would provide all the aid that is needed. Past experience, however, indicates that this is not how nations generally operate. Nations often ignore harms that they have caused, instead choosing to focus on harms that others (usually the enemy) have caused. Moreover, meeting the needs of others under something like the BRP does not seem to be a particularly pressing concern for most nations.

Despite a fair degree of pessimism that would have to accompany any effort to change state practices, the proposals presented in the last two chapters are the best candidates for meeting the basic rights of others. The HP and the BRP both state that nations have certain moral obligation to those in need, and these obligations should be pursued before a nation chooses to pursue other objectives. I return to this idea when I compare an alien admission system based on the HP and the BRP with present policy in Chapter 10. Both the HP and the BRP avoid open-ended obligations. Although the amount of special obligations that a nation will incur under the HP will expand depending on the amount of harm a nation has caused, this is presumably something within a nation's control. In this chapter I have stressed the importance of a nation doing its part in meeting the basic rights of others, but I have also stressed the idea of limiting these moral obligations. Under the notion of Fair Share, a nation's moral obligations are not dependent on others meeting their own obligations. Finally, the notion of Fair Share will set a floor that will provide more assistance to those in need than current practice.

NOTES

1. Henry Shue, "Exporting Hazards," *Ethics* 91 (1981): 603.
2. Samuel Huntington, "Foreign Aid: For What and For Whom?" in Robert Hunter and John Reilly, eds., *Development Today* (New York: Praeger, 1972), 32.
3. Atle Grahl-Madsen, "Refugees and Refugee Law in a World of Transition," *Transnational Legal Problems of Refugees, 1982 Michigan Yearbook of International Legal Studies* (New York: Clark Boardman Company, Ltd., 1982), 74. One important point not raised by Grahl-Madsen is the unemployment rates in the receiving society. As the aborted guest-worker programs in Western Europe show, policymakers will be quite sensitive to such domestic considerations in admitting "strangers." This is not to say that aliens do in fact take the jobs of citizens; the empirical evidence is unclear. What is more clear is that there is this perception.
4. Ibid.

5. One point not raised in Grahl-Madsen's formula is that apart from such variables as GNP per capita or population, certain refugees might be more disruptive in particular societies than others. One can easily think of long-standing ethnic, religious, or racial differences that might make refugee resettlement in certain countries next to impossible. This was one of the critiques I had of Ackerman's "Z" cut-off. This is not to say that mathematical formulas are useless in this area, but it does point out the uncertain and volatile nature of such undertakings.

Chapter 9
A Chapter of Examples

In this chapter I will use a series of examples, some real, some thinly-disguised real world examples, and some hypothetical, in order to better explain the alien admission system towards which I am working.

REAL WORLD EXAMPLES

Mexican Migration

There has been a definite move to increase the number of Mexicans who can legally be admitted to the United States for permanent residence.[1] I do not question this as a policy matter as much as I question the theoretical foundation for this increased migration. I am particularly interested in issues concerning Mexican migration because many of them have been based on the notion that the United States has harmed Mexicans in the past, and/or is currently causing harm. Because the Harm Principle (HP) is such a central part of my theory for alien admissions, the stated rationales for increased Mexican migration need close scrutiny.

Judith Lichtenberg has recently argued in favor of increased alien admission from Mexico based on four criteria: (1) geographic contiguity, (2) the fact that parts of the United States were once a part of Mexico, (3) the fact that the United States has encouraged (or at least not strongly discouraged) Mexicans to migrate here so U.S. employers and consumers could take advantage of a cheap source of labor, and (4) the amount of direct investment in Mexico by U.S. principals.[2]

Gerald Lopez has similarly argued in favor of recognizing a special duty to admit Mexicans to this country.[3] Lopez's argument is difficult to tie down because he seems to fluctuate between seeing a duty to those Mexicans who have come to work in the United States on the one hand, and a duty to Mexicans quite generally. As a result, Lopez's analysis is never entirely clear in terms of what the basis of this preference for Mexicans should be. The fuzziness in his analysis can be seen in a hypothetical example that he employs. Lopez states that if we assumed that there were a certain number of secondary jobs available to foreign workers in the United States, would the American public think those jobs should go to Mexicans or Pakistan nationals? (Lopez assumes that the Pakistanis are poorer than Mexicans, and that the American public would know this). Lopez answers the question by saying that most Americans would say that Mexicans should get these jobs based on the notion that Mexico is our neighbor, we have exploited them, and so on.

I agree with Lopez's prediction in this particular example, but I am not sure what this really tells us. The problem with this approach is that it mixes the descriptive with the prescriptive. However, I am not even sure that it accurately presents the descriptive. It is also quite possible that Mexicans would possibly lose such a popularity contest to British subjects or to Haitian boat people, or to South Vietnamese boat people, or to Salvadorans. It is even more possible that as a theoretical question most Americans would simply want to keep out all foreign workers; so perhaps Lopez's original premise should just be discarded.

As a theoretical proposition, Lopez's discussion, and Lichtenberg's as well, show how notions of restitution can become entangled with notions of "neighborhood." I think it is essential to keep the two ideas separate because they address two different issues. Restitution is based on a special moral obligation to others. Notions of neighborhood are not premised on such special obligations. That is to say, I do not think that geographic contiguity, or the notion of neighborhood, gives rise to a special relationship the way that causing harm to individuals in other societies does.

Perhaps the gravest problem with the Lichtenberg-Lopez analysis is the way in which "harm" has been framed. It is not as if Lichtenberg and Lopez are assuming a general principle of harm and then touching on the borderline or harder cases. Instead, they are looking at the phenomena of illegal Mexican migration to the United States and they are claiming that this is justified because of the "harm" (in addition to neighborhood considerations, see discussion above) caused by the United States. What this completely overlooks is the fact that there might be individuals from other nations who have been harmed even more. In addition, there is no attempt to single out any particular Mexicans as being harmed. Instead, this kind of analysis treats all Mexican claims as virtually one and the same. I argue that there will be individuals who do in fact possess stronger claims for admission to the United Stated than the great bulk of Mexicans who migrate to this country. There will also be some Mexican nationals who will have a stronger claim for admission to the United States than other Mexicans. To argue these points I will take a closer look at the claims that Judith Lichtenberg sets forth.

I will begin with Lichtenberg's first rationale: geographic contiguity. While no one could debate the fact that Mexico borders the United States, several other nations could also make the claim of physical proximity.[4] In addition, one does not have moral obligations only to those who are in geographic proximity. Lichtenberg's second rationale is that parts of the United States were once a part of Mexico. However, one could also point to the fact that parts of the United States were, at one time, owned by Britain, France, Spain and so on.

In addition, Lichtenberg's argument goes back a fair period of time. The passage of time raises some noteworthy issues. On the one hand, moral philosophy usually only attempts to hold individuals responsible for the harms they themselves have caused. This is at the base of the HP. It is this feature that sharply distinguishes the HP from the Basic Rights Principle (BRP). There is an understandable hesitancy, then, to hold individuals responsible for harms caused by an earlier generation of their countrymen. Balanced against this, however, is the idea that restitution should be made for past harms. The key is whether there is a continuing harm or not. To use Shue's example of the Dutch agricultural policy in Java, this example seems to be an instance of a continuing harm because the disastrous consequences are still being felt. Moreover, it is not necessary that the Dutch are still benefiting, or even that they ever did benefit. The key is the harm that has been caused. In the Mexican example we are not speaking of the same levels of harm, nor do we seem to be speaking of a continuing harm.

To go out of order, Lichtenberg's fourth rationale—the amount of direct investment in Mexico by U.S. principals—seems irrelevant to the question of alien admissions. One could easily think of many other instances of direct investment, such as Japanese and Saudi investment in the United States. Would this give American citizens a special right to migrate to these lands? I hardly see the connection.

Finally, we get to Lichtenberg's third rationale—the fact that the United States has encouraged Mexicans to migrate here so U.S. employees and consumers could take advantage of a cheap source of labor. I think this is Lichtenberg's only colorable rationale; but even here the claim in question seems to be a weak one in terms of the moral obligation that arises. To begin with, it is not clear how Mexicans have been harmed in coming to the United States. In fact, the argument that is usually made is that what attracts most Mexicans to the United States are the high wage differentials between these two countries. In other words, Mexicans who come to work here generally improve their position in life. The fact that American consumers also benefit (but some American workers do not) is not germane to our present analysis. American consumers benefit from low wages in many parts of the world. Unless some direct harm can be shown to these workers, or to those societies in general, we should not be invoking the HP. It is also doubtful that many of the Mexicans coming to the United States would fit BRP criteria. The empirical data here are weak, but at least some economists have argued that it is more the differences in wages, rather than Mexicans being on the edge of subsistence, that causes migration to the United States.[5] This is an unsettled question. In any event, if the demographic projections noted earlier do in fact come true, and if the Mexican economy cannot expand to meet the needs of a burgeoning population, then we might see the BRP invoked in the future. The point to stress here, however, is that aid would be given under the weaker BRP and not the HP.

There are stronger rationales for increased migration than Lichtenberg gives. One argument would be that there is an implicit contract between the United States (or various U.S. communities) and Mexico. That is to say, the United States and Mexico (or we could bring it down to a lower level of analysis—individual Mexican workers and U.S. communities and corporations) have an understanding that Mexicans will be allowed to work in this country relatively unfettered. Although I do not think that a nation can supercede its HP and BRP obligations to individuals in other countries by making these kinds of contracts, a nation might well want to meet manpower needs in this way after meeting its prior obligations.

Perhaps the strongest rationale for not excluding or deporting Mexicans who have worked and lived in the United States for a period of time is that they are no longer strangers but fellow members. Note that this does not say that *all* Mexicans reach this status, or even those with a fleeting relationship with the American community. The legalization provisions in Simpson-Mazzoli recognize that it would be unfair (and impractical if not impossible) to return aliens to their home country when they have a longstanding relationship with this country.

To summarize on the question of Mexican migration, the point that I have been making in this section is that those who have argued for increased Mexican migration have generally done so without looking at the claims of individuals in other countries, nor have they been discerning enough among the variety of claims presented by Mexicans. In addition, arguments about harm have become intertwined with those of being neighbors. As a result, special obligations have been mixed with general obligations and even preferences. A closer examination of the "harm" done to Mexican migrants, generally, fails to find a harm that brings about the same moral obligations as those we will later examine. The biggest flaw, then, in the Lichtenberg-Lopez analysis is the lack of harm. One reason for this result is that the claims of Mexicans have not been compared with those from other societies.

All of this is not to say that Mexicans will not continue to come to this country. As long as wage differences are so large between the two countries, and as long as large numbers of people in the United States benefit from such migration, there will probably always be some form of de facto alien admissions.[6] What I have stressed here, however, is that that the moral claims of Mexicans might not be as strong as some philosophers make them out to be.

Not all arguments for increased migration to the United States based on some notion of harm have been about Mexican migration. Elsa Chaney has argued that the United States has a special duty to admit aliens in countries where the U.S. sponsored Public Health Service has reduced the death rates, thus causing overpopulation.[7] Using the same kind of logic, Antonio Pido has sought to establish the proposition that because the United States has helped to establish an educational system in the Philippines that has made for an overeducated society, the United States has an obligation to admit some of these high achievers.[8]

I do not find either Chaney's or Pido's arguments at all persuasive. Neither presents a particularly compelling argument that a serious harm has occurred. Moreover, the practical result of Chaney's logic would be to severely restrict the humanitarian aid that a nation would give. That is to say that a nation that is saddled with having to take in aliens from nations that it is attempting to aid might soon find the more desirable route is not to give any aid. The argument seems strangely counterproductive, besides being counterintuitive. The fact that these other nations are autonomous and sovereign places a heavy burden on them to care for their own citizenry. I use Pido's argument for no other reason than to show how easy it is for some to manufacture a possible Harm Principle violation, and why it is necessary that we be quite careful in only honoring the most severe and compelling instances of harm.

War

Vietnam. In some respects the U.S. military involvement in Vietnam would be a prototype of the HP.[9] One nation intervenes in another nation in pursuit of certain foreign policy goals and in the process it "harms" noncombatants in another society. The harm comes not only from the physical harm or death that it brought on, but there has also been a severe infringement on Vietnamese society more generally.[10] I will not focus on what actions the United States took to prevent harm during the war. Instead, my concern is with U.S. activities after the war. That is, because of the vast destruction of life and property we can assume harm for purposes of the HP. The more interesting and pressing question involves the issue of resettlement in this country after the war. The U.S. has admitted over 700,000 Vietnamese since the fall of Saigon in 1975. It might be argued that through its large-scale refugee resettlement program the United States is recognizing some special duty to the Vietnamese.[11] I turn now to see if such actions have in fact been warranted, and if those who have been admitted have had the strongest claim for admission.

In Chapter 7 I argued that in instances of war the HP makes a distinction between combatants and noncombatants. The former accept the risks of war while the latter do not. There is a special duty to protect and aid noncombatants but not the combatants. Using this criterion, the U.S. Vietnamese resettlement program does not fare well. The first wave of Vietnamese refugees in 1975 was by no means a cross section of Vietnamese society, nor were those admitted war innocents. Instead, admission criteria was dependent on some connection with the United States, defined in terms of: family connections, former employment with the U.S. government, or former employment with a U.S. corporation. Those admitted in this first wave were the high ranking military and civilian leaders and so on.[12]

Although Vietnamese refugee resettlement continued throughout the 1970s, it was not until 1979 that the second wave of refugees began to come to this country. At its height over 14,000 refugees per month were arriving at U.S. shores. Vietnamese refugee resettlement is still a phenomenon very much with us today, although the numbers have steadily decreased.[13] It should be noted that those coming into the United States since 1979 have represented more of a cross section of Vietnamese society than the first wave of migrants. Despite this egalitarian trend,[14] there is evidence that those who will linger in the refugee camps for years are those who are somehow less "desirable."[15] I do not offer this as proof that those who linger in the squalor of these camps necessarily have the strongest claim for admission based on our present discussion, but the apparent upper-class bias to our refugee resettlement program is indeed quite puzzling, and frankly quite disconcerting.

The discussion so far has shown that U.S. refugee resettlement efforts in Vietnam have not sufficiently followed a combatant/noncombatant distinction. It seems quite likely that policymakers felt an affinity to military leaders and political leaders, although it is doubtful if this affinity has been shared by the American public. It also seems quite likely that there has been a concerted effort to show that the United States does not desert its friends. Although honoring affinities is commendable, a nation should not use its affinities, or purported affinities, to obscure or avoid more pressing moral obligations.

Marshall Cohen has stated that apparent conflicts between moral and political concerns often disappear when more complex moral criteria are applied:

> It is because the realist fails to appreciate the fact of moral conflict, or to understand that we are sometimes morally justified in defaulting on our obligations, in violating the rights of others, or, more generally, in doing dark and terrible things, that he develops a "political" justification for doing them. From this "realistic," political point of view he often criticizes the naiveté of the moralist's political thinking. But the fault lies rather in the simplicity of his own view of morality.[16]

Some might argue that the Vietnamese refugee program is exactly the kind of thing that Cohen is talking about here: we need to overlook the moral obligations we have to noncombatants in order to meet some stronger moral obligation, or to promote some stronger moral principle, such as the idea of helping war allies when they are in need. I am not convinced that the Vietnamese resettlement program meets this standard of achieving some higher or more complex moral ideal. Cohen's analysis should not be used so that nations seek to achieve political ends under some purported higher or more complex moral standard.

It is possible to make an even stronger charge against the Vietnamese resettlement policy: it should never have occurred in the first place, at least not to the extent that it has been carried out. To begin with, it is very noteworthy that admission to the United States came after the war was over. At that time the threat of death for many was greatly lessened. This is not to ignore the fact that during the war build-up there was a continual discussion of a bloodbath should the North win. This might explain admission (for some) immediately after the war, but surely that rationale cannot be used at the present time. My position also does not ignore the brutality of the war and the heavy damage caused by the United States; nor does it ignore the duty to make some restitution for these harmful activities. Moreover, I assume that there is a continuing harm in Vietnam from our activities during the war. What I question is the form of restitution. The sounder explanation for the actions of the United States after 1975 is that the United States is in the process of making some foreign policy points through this refugee program (much as it has with Cuban migration),[17] combined with some sort of national guilt for our war activities. I would argue that the basis for our refugee program has not been well thought out, and that it has ignored far more efficient and less disruptive means of making restitution to those we have harmed.

This is not to say that admission for some would not be warranted. *During* the hostilities I think it might have been possible to save a great many noncombatant lives by some type of temporary admission system. The grounding for such a policy would have been the HP. We had a duty to protect civilian lives. Immediately after the war we might have given admission to those whose lives appeared endangered: high ranking generals and so on. However, the basis for such aid would not have been the HP because these individuals freely accepted the consequences of fighting in a war. Instead such aid would have been premised on the BRP. These people are in serious need and we recognize their basic right to subsistence.

As a general rule, then, I am not convinced that the large-scale refugee resettlement that we have promoted in Vietnam is morally obligatory. At the present time those who have been sent to reeducation camps are now getting preferred admission to the United States.[18] Although the behavior of the ruling regime in Vietnam cannot be excused, we need to be precise about the basis for our aid to those who spent time in these camps.[19] Assuming the threshold level of harm is met, I would argue that admission for these individuals would have to be premised on the BRP rather than the HP. Like the first wave of refugees in 1975, those currently getting to the head of the line were formerly high ranking government officials. Again these are individuals who freely accepted the harm that war might bring to them. Aid might be warranted for this group, but it is important that we first honor our obligations to those we have harmed, those who did not freely accept the consequences of war.

An excellent example of aiding those we have harmed would be Amerasian children. This group is also getting preferred admission, but these claims are much stronger than those examined above.[20] It is important to note that the rationale for preferred admission for this group is that (1) these are war innocents who were the victims of our actions in that country,[21] (2) these individuals have been singled out for persecution, and (3) other forms of assistance would prove ineffective. The fact of American blood, by itself, is not compelling, although one might explain the concern to admit these youngsters more on the basis of an affinity than a recognition of a moral obligation.

To close this section I want to reiterate that I recognize the very strong obligation that the United States owes to certain sectors of Vietnamese society for the "harm" that the United States caused in the pursuit of its war goals. However, I am not convinced that admission to this country is the restitution that is warranted. Moreover, the way that we have carried out our resettlement program raises a lot of questions. For example, we have used the family reunification principle to determine which individuals should get preferred admission to our country, but it is our definition of family, not the Vietnamese definition.[22] The fact that those who remain in refugee camps for years are from the lowest rung of Vietnamese society is also questionable. Finally, admission to this nation has been accomplished at the expense, sometimes quite literally, of many subcommunities in the United States which often had no forewarning of large-scale resettlement plans, and even fewer resources to cope with such a communal disorder.[23] In sum, the Vietnamese refugee resettlement program has had a number of theoretical and practical flaws.

El Salvador. A sharp contrast to the large-scale admission of Vietnamese is the attempted exclusion of those leaving El Salvador. It is estimated that there are upwards of 500,000 Salvadorans in the United States illegally.[24] In 1983 only 3 percent of the Salvadorans in this country who applied for asylum status were granted it.[25] The United Nations's Office of the High Commissioner for Refugees (UNHCR) has recognized that many of those fleeing El Salvador are bona fide refugees,[26] and this office has been quite critical of U.S. activities in this area quite generally.[27] The United States has obviously disagreed with the UNHCR on the status of Salvadorans, and this is reflected both in the asylum statistics noted earlier, and in the fact that the government has begun a crackdown on those offering private asylum to Salvadorans.[28]

Assistant Secretary of State Elliot Abrams describes the rationale behind the policy of the United States in these terms:

There are dozens of wars, civil wars and insurgencies in the world today, and almost all in the third world.... Those who ask that all Salvadorans be allowed to stay in the United States indefinitely must explain why the same treatment is not deserved by all other migrants from poor, violent societies to our South—now and in coming years.[29]

What is so puzzling about the government's rationale is that it completely ignores U.S. activities in El Salvador. In fact, this statement seems to offer no distinction in terms of U.S. relations with other nations to our south. Instead, those below our borders are treated as indistinguishable "banana republics" in the most pejorative sense of that term. Abrams's remarks conveniently ignore the fact that the United States has provided very heavy military support for a war that has produced between 40,000–50,000 *civilian* deaths.[30]

It might be argued that, unlike Vietnam, U.S. military involvement in El Salvador is only indirect. Given the brutality of the war in El Salvador, particularly the astounding number of civilian deaths, I do not think the United States can ignore an obligation to those who have been severely harmed just because the United States is not directly causing harm. That is to say, the United States has been providing aid where it knows that great "harm" is likely to occur, and where little effort has been made to protect civilians from this harm. This is not to say that any time one nation provides weapons to another country, and civilians ultimately are harmed, that the nation providing weapons will bear some special obligation. However, in the context of El Salvador we have a situation where the U.S. government knows full well the kind of harm that is being caused, and it persists in continuing to provide support in increasing amounts that perpetuates this state of affairs.

It might also be argued that the brutal treatment of civilians in El Salvador would exist even without the economic and military support of the U.S. government. Assuming for the sake of argument that this is true, the fact that the United States continues to supply large quantities of military weapons to a government that must bear a large burden of the responsibility for these widespread civilian killings would still implicate the United States to some degree. I am not at all convinced, however, that there would be the same level of killing of civilians absent the military support provided by the United States.

What duty does the United States have? Because of its support for this brutal civil war in El Salvador, the United States has a special duty to protect noncombatants and a special duty to aid those who have been harmed by the war. One means of protecting noncombatants would be to offer protection within El Salvador, although such efforts have had dismal consequences.[31] Another alternative, one that I think should be seriously considered, would be for the United States to admit Saldavoran noncombatants who are truly fleeing the civil war until such time that the danger to civilians reasonably subsides. Determining whether individuals are honestly fleeing the war or merely seeking economic gain has no easy solution. Given the past practices of both sides in this civil conflict, I would say that if we were to err we should err in a liberal manner: it is human life that we are considering. This is also to say what should seem rather obvious: current U.S. asylum practice, as it applies to Salvadorans, is a sham.[32] Moreover, the U.S. government should not forcibly deport Salvadorans in this country who are fearful for their lives if sent back to El Salvador. The present administration has broken a long standing precedent by denying Salvadorans Extended Voluntary Departure (EVD) status.[33] This administrative process allows otherwise deportable aliens to remain in the United States until violent conditions in the home country subside. Finally, the government should end its current crackdown on those providing Sanctuary for Salvadorans.[34]

Subsistence/Persecution

In 1980 over 10,000 Haitian "boat people" came to the United States illegally. Perhaps what prompted this sudden influx was the fact that at the same time the U.S. government was welcoming over 125,000 Cubans "with open arms."[35] Seventy percent of the Haitian population desperately attempts to live on a per capita income of less than $150 a year. The average life span in that country is fifty years. State Department reports conflict in terms of whether there is political persecution in Haiti. In 1979 the United States admitted 6433 Haitians through its normal flow immigration channels.[36] Of those declaring occupations, 14.6 percent were either professionals, or managers and administrators.[37] This contrasts with the fact that only 1 percent of the Haitian population falls into that category of workers.[38] The socioeconomic background of normal flow immigrants also sharply contrasts with the socioeconomic backgrounds of the Haitian boat people.[39]

The Haitian boat people who came to this country in 1980 have almost universally been denied asylum, although few, if any, have been returned to Haiti. Their situation in this country is uncertain. The United States government has sought to prevent any more illegal migration. The Coast Guard has been working in tandem with the Haitian government to return boats with human cargo in them.[40]

What are the duties of a country like the United States, either to those Haitians who came to the United States in 1980, or to Haitians generally? The first level of analysis is to see if the United States has pursued actions that have caused harm to the Haitian population. The answer seems to be no, although some point to the U.S. military occupation from 1915–1934 and claim that this caused serious harm to the Haitian population.[41]

It might also be argued that the United States had been instrumental in maintaining both "Papa Doc" Duvalier and his son, the recently deposed "Baby Doc," in power, and that as a result the United States is implicated in the unjust practices of both rulers. I make no pretense to being a Haitian scholar. My purpose is not to give a full-blown account of Haitian politics (or the politics of any other country under discussion), but to show how an analysis of moral responsibilities should be worked out. My own conclusions on what has occurred in other countries, in some respects, should be the least important concern. The method of analysis and the grounding of moral obligations are my true aims. However, I think it is essential to begin to debate these issues and not simply accept the seductive notion that moral concerns should play no role in the international arena. In the present instance, my own reasonably informed guess is that both Duvalier regimes have been grossly unjust. One would be hard pressed to read Judge King's opinion in the *Haitian Refugee Center v. Civiletti* (*HRC*) case and think otherwise. However, I also fail to see where the United States should be implicated in the unjustness of this regime.[42]

Assuming, for the sake of discussion, that the United States has not harmed Haiti for purposes of the HP, the next question is whether the United States would have any moral obligation under the BRP. The fact that 70 percent of the Haitian population has a per capita income less than $150 per year would seem to strongly suggest that many individuals are on the edge of subsistence. Because of this, part of the United States's Fair Share might well go to helping these destitute Haitians. Because assistance should precede admission as a general rule, reflecting the disruptive effect that admission will oftentimes bring, it might be possible to meet a BRP obligation to Haiti without having to admit any Haitians to our country.

Starvation, however, is not the only threat to the basic rights of the Haitian population. For some Haitian citizens life in Haiti is filled with terror. In Judge King's very moving opinion in the *HRC* case the situation is described this way:

> In reaching its conclusions the court has listened to a wealth of in-court testimony, examined numerous depositions, and read hundreds of documents submitted by the parties. Much of the evidence is both shocking and brutal, populated by the ghosts of individuals Haitians—including those who have been returned from the United States—who have been beaten, tortured and left to die in Haitian prisons.[43]

What obligations would a country like the United States have to those who are the targets of persecution by the government or the Tonton Macoutes? Walzer's response would be to tolerate at least some of this persecution in order to respect the autonomy of other societies, and to allow other countries to develop in their own way. As I stated earlier, given military intervention as a sole alternative, other nations are well advised to tread slowly and softly. I am not convinced, however, that military intervention is the only solution or the best one. I would urge that a country like the United States should work to meet the basic rights of individuals who do suffer severe persecution at the hands of the Haitian government or its agents through a process of alien admissions. In fact, alien admissions might well be the only effective means of protecting the autonomy of individuals singled out for death or persecution. Again, it is important to note that assuming no U.S. complicity, any aid would be based under the BRP rather than the HP. As a result, if the United States chose to meet its BRP obligations in this way it would not be obligated to aid all of those in need.

The physical proximity of Haiti might well promote a more practical concern. Instead of the United States doing its Fair Share on a random or worldwide basis, there might well be some strong policy grounds for instituting a system that would allow a nation to give its Fair Share to its neighbors. In this way, aid would seem to be more manageable in terms of implementation.

In addition, keeping tabs on how assistance money is being spent would seem to be easier than the situation where aid is given to a faraway land.⁴⁴

Unjust Regimes

Chile. It is now no great secret (if there was ever a time when it was a secret) that the United States was very much responsible for the overthrow of the popularly elected Allende regime in Chile.⁴⁵ In place of Allende, Chile has been ruled by the repressive Pinochet regime. With these changes the general Chilean population has been harmed; Chileans, generally, are now forced to live under a regime that does not respect the autonomy of the individual. For its complicity in the coup, the United States has "harmed" Chilean citizens for HP purposes. Some will differ with my position, which is that the Allende regime was much more just than Pinochet's has been. Moreover, the Pinochet regime has been quite severe in its treatment of any dissension. It is this change in regimes, coupled with the U.S. involvement in the overthrow of Allende, that invokes the HP. Although there has been a general harm to the Chilean community, we must also recognize that some citizens have been harmed more than others. Assistance should be made with such distinctions in mind. To meet its obligations under the HP, the United States should admit those who have suffered (or are likely to suffer) from torture and severe persecution. In terms of its duty to the great bulk of the Chilean population—those who "merely" suffer daily indignities—the United States should cease all military assistance, and all economic assistance that would not harm the general population. If, for some reason, the United States can no longer be said to be harming Chile, there could also be a duty to aid those singled out for persecution under the BRP.

Iran. In 1954 the CIA played a major role in overthrowing the Muraddeq regime in Iran and placing the Shah in power.⁴⁶ For many years after this the United States supported this repressive regime by providing it with large sums of money, military weapons, and instruments of terror for the Shah's secret police. Despite such efforts, the Shah was overthrown and the Ayatollah Khomeini has come to power. Khomeini's regime has also been marked by terror, and it has waged an endless war with Iraq that has brought about the death or mutilation of thousands of individuals who are usually thought of as noncombatants.

Has the United States harmed Iran? If the only actions that the United States took were those in 1954, then we would be hard pressed to continue to see a harm at the present time. The rationale for this would be that absent a continuing harm, subsequent generations should not be held responsible for harm done by preceding generations. Of course, U.S. involvement in Iranian affairs did not end in 1954. The United States bears an obligation to the Iranian population for harms it has caused since that time, most noticeably, propping up an unjust regime. Because of its continued support of a regime where there was a great deal of evidence pointing to widespread unjust practices, the United States is generally implicated in these harms to Iranian citizens. What would lessen U.S. responsibility, to a certain extent, is the fact that an unjust regime has followed the Shah. Under these circumstances, it is not possible to say "but for" the actions of the U.S. government (or of any other government) the Iranian population would be living under a just regime. To carry out the analysis, if one finds that the United States is not implicated in the harms to the Iranian people, the United States could still have some duty under the Basic Rights Principle.

HYPOTHETICAL EXAMPLES

War

Countries F and G fight a war and F is victorious. As a result, 500,000 citizens of G flee that country, claiming that they will all be slaughtered by the military of F. Many seek refuge in H, a rich country that was not a part of the war between F and G. What are the duties of H? Country H would not have any duty to the citizens of G under the Harm Principle. That is, H has not taken any action that has caused harm to the citizens of G. We reach this result even though some citizens of H might have an ideological affinity with the citizens of G. This, however, is only the first step in the analysis. We also recognize that individuals have a basic right to subsistence. As a result, H might come to the aid of these citizens (or some of these citizens) under the BRP. What form of aid should H pursue? Again, as a general rule assistance should be given priority over alien admissions. This is to protect ongoing social communities and at the same time to protect individuals in these communities. In addition, the evidence seems to indicate that economic assistance is much more cost effective than alien admissions is.

In the present case, however, if the threat by F is real enough, assistance other than alien admissions would be rather meaningless. Assuming, then, that H decides to meet all of its moral obligations under the BRP with aid to G, how many individuals should H admit? Because H has not harmed citizens of G, H is only obligated to give a Fair Share. In the previous chapter I discussed Grahl-Madsen's formula for dividing up refugee resettlement among the nations of the world and this, or a similar formula, should dictate what H's moral obligation will entail.

Some might argue that there are other motivational problems in this example, and in my approach quite generally. To stay with this example, what would prevent the citizens of G from greatly offending F when it was apparent that G was going to lose the war, thereby increasing the chances of reprisal, but at the same time ensuring that migration to an affluent country like H might be necessary. In fact, it might be argued that for these same reasons G might start a war with F knowing full well that it will lose, but providing citizens in G an excuse to claim possible death at the hands of F, and therefore a need for refuge. This would be "The Mouse That Roared" with a third party, H, involved.

Perhaps my reasoning is too pragmatic, but it seems difficult to imagine citizens in one nation purposely offending another nation so these citizens could migrate elsewhere. For one thing, the assurance of refuge in other countries would be anything but certain. These kinds of occurrences are much more likely in individual circumstances. For example, in *Cistenas-Estay v. INS* the third circuit refused to grant relief to a husband and wife from Chile who claimed they would be persecuted if they were forced to return to their home country.[47] This couple had not suffered persecution while they lived in Chile, but they claimed that they would be faced with persecution after they had staged a well-publicized press conference in Washington, D.C. at which time they denounced the Pinochet regime. The court stated that it would not order relief for such bootstrap refugees. The same kind of reasoning should apply in the instant case. Like the HP, aid under the BRP is not given out simply on the basis that others claim some need. Instead, we need to be very discerning to the claim of need. Those who purposely bring need on themselves are less deserving of our attention.

Subsistence

Country D causes starvation in country E because smokestacks in D have severely polluted E, leaving very little arable land. What duties, if any, would D have to E? This would seem to be a very straightforward HP example. D has taken actions that have severely harmed citizens in another country. Moreover, E has in no way invited such activities.

What type of restitution is warranted? For starters, D should immediately cease its polluting activities. Beyond that, however, we need to consider restitution for both past action and future harm. As I noted earlier, admission to another society should be one of the last—if not *the* last—policy options to follow. We reach this result because communities will only be able to absorb so many new "strangers" without incurring serious negative consequences. It should also be pointed out that individuals in other societies who have been harmed will generally want to remain in their own society. Finally, D could more efficiently aid E through assistance other than admission to D. In this instance, monetary assistance, or direct food aid, seems warranted rather than alien admission. How long does the duty last? If the land in E remains fallow because of D's polluting activities, then there would be a continuing obligation. If the harm dissipates at some point, then so would D's duty.

Change the facts so that instead of causing widespread starvation in E, D's polluting activities caused the GNP of E to fall by 10 percent. Unless citizens in E were on the edge of subsistence, the actions of D would not cause enough "harm" to invoke the HP. E's strongest argument would be that it has not freely accepted or invited this "harm." Although this is true, this fact, by itself, should not be enough to invoke the HP. The HP only seeks to remedy cases of severe harm. This case is not such a situation.

Change the facts so that not only does the GNP of E fall, but a quarter of the population falls below subsistence because of the polluting activities of D. The HP would seem to be invoked under these circumstances. However, what if it were possible for E to redistribute resources domestically so that those who had fallen below subsistence are brought above subsistence? This makes for a much more difficult question to answer. Under these circumstances we would not meet the required threshold of harm to invoke the HP. Therefore the HP does not apply (of course, neither would the BRP). One of the unsettling aspects of this decision is that D has seemingly violated the autonomy of E without having to make restitution. Perhaps this example shows the limited applicability of the HP, the incomplete nature of morality at the international level, and the need, at times, to go beyond the HP. This, however, is beyond the enterprise I have undertaken. My purpose is to only look at instances of serious harm, and after E's actions there is none, although the motivational problems should be apparent.

Another difficult hypothetical situation to address would be where E has invited D to pursue activities in E, which in turn causes this pollution, which then causes this drop in GNP and destitution for some. Perhaps D dumped nuclear waste in E and there were spills and leaks. What kind of duty would D have under these circumstances? It is important to balance a number of competing claims here. On the one hand, we seek to respect the autonomy of E. As a result, when E invites another nation to do business we will treat this "as if" these activities were being performed by E in a domestic capacity. We also noted, however, that sometimes invited nations need to take special precautions to ensure that individuals in other societies are not harmed.

I have argued that when there is the potential for great harm and it appears as if ineffective means will be taken to prevent this harm by the host nation, then the invited nation will have some duty to ensure that harm does not occur. Even if the host nation will in fact take special pains to ensure that no harm arises, some activities may be so inherently dangerous that other nations should not be allowed to take such risks. Perhaps nuclear waste is such an example; I will only raise this question. It is this idea, combined with the fact that some other nations might be virtually coerced to accept such risks because of their poverty and very poor bargaining position, that makes agreements such as the one in this example so suspect. In this case, special precautions should be taken by D to ensure that E has not contracted to accept nuclear waste out of desperation, and that the handling of this material will be performed in a safe manner.

Notice how the HP changes the duties of nations. Under a "trustee" view D would have little if any duty to take special precautions to protect the citizens of E. Under the HP, instead, a nation like D will have some duty, depending on the circumstances, to ensure the safety of the citizens of E. A final matter would be whether E is a just regime or not. Under my definition, an unjust regime will not look out for the best interests of its citizens. A regime that exhibits little concern for the well being of its own citizens cannot be expected to be concerned that other countries will either. Under these situations, a nation like D might have to take some steps to ensure the safety of E's citizens. In the present case there is no evidence either way on this question.

Subsistence and Unjust Regimes

Through forces of nature, country M is experiencing a severe drought. As a result, all eight million of its people are on the verge of starvation. What would be the duty of N, an affluent country, to the citizens of M? In this case, although there is indisputably great need in M, N has not caused it. Therefore there is no reason to invoke the HP. This much should be clear. We reach this result even if N has the capability of feeding all of the citizens of M. Of course, this does fully address the question of N's obligations. N, and nations like N, will have some obligation to meet the basic rights of those starving. If N has already given its Fair Share in assistance (or taken in the agreed upon number of refugees), then it has met its obligations under the BRP. Any aid beyond this would be charity, but charity that should be encouraged to meet short-term crises.

Change these facts so that 80 percent of the population in M is starving while the other 20 percent, the ruling elite, is living quite well, refusing to provide aid to their compatriots, and actually siphoning off aid. What are the duties of other societies? Some might argue that the actions of this 20 percent would absolve outsiders from giving aid. After all, if countrymen won't assist, why should foreigners? In addition, it looks as if aid would not do any good anyway. I would argue against such a position based on the idea that an individual's basic rights should not be ignored because others are not honoring them, whether these other individuals are in the same society or not.

Change the facts so that nation N is supporting this ruling regime in M by supplying weapons that terrorize the population. As a result of these actions, N is harming M and the HP would be invoked. Defining exactly what degree of support is necessary to invoke the HP is not easy. There are a number of possible means of providing aid: the sale of military weapons, economic assistance, training the militia of another nation, and so on. If it appears as if the aid that is given is significant in maintaining this regime in power, then a nation like N would be implicated. The form that assistance takes would be important in arriving at this determination. For example, if a nation was providing instruments of terror to an unjust regime it would be easier to conclude that the nation providing such "aid" is helping to harm those persecuted. A more difficult situation is economic aid. Generally such assistance does not harm anyone. However, if it could be shown that the economic assistance that a nation was providing was being used to buy instruments of terror, to use the most obvious example, then the sending nation would be implicated in the affairs of this unjust regime, assuming it knew or should have known of such practices. The presumption in favor of respecting the autonomy of other nations is rebutted when a nation systematically ignores the basic human rights of its citizens. This is the situation presented here.

Another difficult question is how best to aid the 80 percent in N who are starving. If the regime in N did not siphon off this aid the answer would be straightforward: provide food and economic assistance. Because of the unjust actions of the ruling regime such aid would not meet the serious needs of this population. Moreover, it seems unlikely that alien admissions would be the best means of meeting these needs—given the large numbers of people that we will presume this would involve.[48] Instead, under these types of situations the proper response might be military intervention—preferably by an international force—to overthrow this unjust regime. Again, it needs to be pointed out that there are a number of rather extreme situations here that seem to dictate this result: an unjust regime that is taking all of the foreign aid sent to the country, the very large numbers of individuals who are starving, and the fact that alien admissions (or other forms of assistance) would not seem to be a very effective means of meeting the needs of these people.

CONCLUSION

I have attempted to give added insight into the HP and the BRP by showing how these principles could be applied to several real world and hypothetical examples. One striking note is how infrequently the HP is recognized by nations that are causing harm to others. Focus on Chile. Few would deny the role played by the United States in the overthrow of Allende. Perhaps fewer still would deny that Pinochet's regime is unjust. However, nowhere have I seen it suggested that the United States owes any special obligation to those who have suffered severe persecution at the hands of this regime. Does this mean that the HP is lacking as a theoretical model? Obviously I would strongly disagree. What is needed, I believe, are much stronger efforts to get nations to recognize and admit to harms that they have caused. If this is not forthcoming, then other nations and nongovernmental organizations need to be more vigilant in not only pointing out instances of harm, but the cause of this harm as well.

NOTES

1. Prior to 1985 the Simpson-Mazzoli legislation would have allowed for increased migration for Mexico by allowing contiguous nations (Mexico and Canada) to used unused visas of the other nation from

the previous year. This year's version of this legislation, S. 1200 and H.R. 3080, are without these provisions.

2. Judith Lichtenberg, "Mexican Migration and U. S. Policy: A Guide for the Perplexed," in Peter Brown and Henry Shue, eds., *The Border That Joins: Mexican Migrants and U.S. Responsibility* (Totowa, N.J.: Rowman and Littlefield, 1983).

3. Gerald Lopez, "Undocumented Mexican Migration: In Search of a Just Immigration Law and Policy," *U.C.L.A. Law Review* 28 (1981): 615–714.

4. This argument was made continuously in debate on the Caribbean Basin Initiative. See *Cong. Rec.*, Dec. 12, 1982, H.10123–10168.

5. See David North and Marion Houstoun, "The Characteristics and Role of Illegal Aliens in the U.S. Labor Market: An Exploratory Study," reprinted in *Selected Readings on U.S. Immigration Policy and Law* (Washington, D.C.: GPO, 1980); see also Wayne Cornelius, "Illegal Mexican Migration," in that same volume.

6. One reason for the lack of control over our national borders is the incompetency in the immigration service itself. See Milton D. Morris, *Immigration—The Beleagured Bureaucracy* (Washington, D.C.: Brookings Institute, 1985). For a darker side of the INS see John Crewdson, *The Tarnished Door: The New Immigrants and the Transformation of America* (New York: Times Books, 1983).

7. Elsa Chaney, "Migrant Workers and National Boundaries: The Basis for Rights and Protections," in Peter Brown and Henry Shue, eds., *Boundaries: National Autonomy and Its Limits* (Totowa, N.J.: Rowman and Littlefield, 1981).

8. Antonio J. A. Pido, "Brain Drain Philippines," *Society* 14 (1977): 50–53. The Report of the Interagency Task Force on Immigration Policy likewise pointed to a feeling by Filipinos that they should get preference over other countries in migrating to the United States because of the past colonial relationship to this country. *Staff Report*, Departments of Justice, Labor and State, U.S. Interagency Task Force on Immigration Policy, (Washington, D.C.: GPO, 1979), 292.

9. My comments only address the question of the claims of those from Vietnam. A similar kind of analysis could be done for other Southeast Asian groups. A good start would be with William Shawcross's book *Sideshow: Kissinger, Nixon and the Destruction of Cambodia* (New York: Pocket Books, 1979).

10. See generally Arnold Isaacs, *Without Honor: Defeat in Vietnam and Cambodia* (Baltimore: Johns Hopkins University Press, 1983).

11. Occasionally, however, the U.S. government will act as if it does not possess any special obligation. This attitude is reflected in language

from a factfinding tour of Southeast Asia. "In fact, the UNHCR has met with little success in its efforts to seek a more equitable sharing of the resettlement burden [Southeast Asians]. Some regions of the world, such as Latin America, have consistently refused to participate. Developing countries in such areas must be encouraged—through vigorous miltilateral and bilateral efforts—to accept their resettlement responsibilities." U.S. Cong., House, Committee on the Judiciary, *Refugee Issues in Southeast Asia and Europe and International Issues on Drug Enforcement and Administrative Law*, 97th Cong., 2nd sess., (1982), 7.

12. See generally Gail Paradise Kelly, *From Vietnam to America* (Boulder: Westview Press, 1977), chapters 2 and 3; William Liu, *Transition to Nowhere* (Nashville: Charter House Publisher, 1979).

13. In 1980 215,000 refugees were admitted to the United States (not counting the 135,000 Cuban/Haitian "entrants"); in 1981 159,000 refugees were brought here. Since that time the numbers have steadily diminished. In 1982 97,000 refugees came to the United States. In 1983 there was an approval for 90,000 refugees, but only 60,000 came to this country. Finally, in 1984 72,000 slots have been approved, although the number admitted should be much smaller. See the Report to Congress, *Refugee Resettlement Program*, published by the Office of Refugee Resettlement for years 1981 through 1984. Also see "U.S. Sets Limits on Refugees," *New York Times*, Sept. 27, 1983, 3.

14. The empirical evidence on this is not clear. A recent study by the Office of Refugee Resettlement reported in the *New York Times* found that 56.5 percent of the resettled refugees from Vietnam had held white collar jobs in their homeland. (Judith Cummings, "Resettlement of 455,000 in U.S. Viewed as a Success," Sept. 16, 1984, 12). To my knowledge, this kind of data has only been used to gauge how well the Vietnamese are being settled. For example, this study found that only 27.1 percent of the resettled refugees held white collar jobs in the United States. Obviously I look at this data another way. I question whether we are truly meeting our moral obligation to the Vietnamese when those admitted have such a spectacular socioeconomic background, while those lingering in refugee camps are of the lower strata.

15. Astri Suhrke, "Indochinese Refugees: The Law and Politics of Asylum," in *The Annals of the American Academy of Political and Social Sciences*, Special Ed. Gilbert Loescher and John Scanlan (Beverly Hills: Sage, 1983); see also Steve Lohr, "At Camp Hilton in Philippines, Vietnamese Learn U.S. Ways," *New York Times*, Sept. 22, 1984, 6.

16. Marshall Cohen, "Moral Skepticism and International Relations," *Philosophy and Public Affairs* 13 (1984): 306.

17. Michael Teitelbaum shares this view: "From the perspective of

the receiving countries, refugee admission policies have been guided in many important cases by the belief that refugee outflows serve to embarrass and discredit adversary nations. Such a belief has surely been central to U.S. policies toward migrants from Cuba, Vietnam and the Soviet Union." "Immigration, Refugees and Foreign Policy," *International Organization* 38 (1984): 439.

18. See Bernard Gwertzman, "More Vietnamese to Get Permission to Enter the U.S.," *New York Times* Sept. 12, 1984, 1; Barbara Crossette, "Exiles Tell of Stark Life in Vietnam Prisons," *New York Times*, Sept. 16, 1984, 1.

19. See Stephen Young, "The Legality of Vietnamese Education Camps," *Harvard International Law Journal* 20 (1979): 519–38.

20. See Nan Robertson, "Amerasian War Orphans Come to U.S.," *New York Times*, Apr. 18, 1984, 1.

21. Victims in the sense that these children were generally abandoned by their GI fathers.

22. Gail Kelly writes: "Many Vietnamese refused to accept sponsorships because they meant family separations. VOLAGs [voluntary agencies] often split extended families into several households and resettled these households in disparate parts of the country." *From Vietnam to America*, 140.

23. See U.S. Cong., House, Hearings before the Subcommittee on Immigration, Refugees, and International Law of the Committee on the Judiciary, *Refugee Assistance*, 98th Cong., 1st sess. (1980).

24. See Bernard Gwertzman, "Salvadorans to Gain Refugee Status," *New York Times*, Sept. 22, 1983, 3.

25. Contrast that with the fact that 78 percent of the Russian applicants, 64 percent of the Ethiopian, and 53 percent of the Afghan applicants were granted asylum. See Arthur C. Helton, "Political Asylum Under the 1980 Refugee Act: An Unfulfilled Promise," *University of Michigan Journal of Law Reform* 17 (1984): 253.

26. Letter from Kallu Kalumiya, Legal Counsel UNHCR, *Re: UNHCR Mandate Definition of Refugee and the Situation of Salvadoran Asylum Seekers*, February, 1982, p. 10.

27. "Recommend that the UNHCR should continue to express its concern to the U.S. government that its apparent failure to grant asylum to any significant number of Salvadorans, coupled with continuing large-scale forcible and voluntary return to El Salvador, would appear to represent a negation of its responsibilities assumed upon its adherence to the Protocol." *United Nations High Commissioner for Refugees, Mission to Monitor INS Asylum Processing of Salvadoran Illegal Entrants*, Sept. 13–18, 1981, reprinted in the *Cong. Rec.*, Feb. 11, 1982, S.827–31.

28. See Wayne King, "9 Plead Not Guilty in Tucson to Smuggling Illegal Aliens," *New York Times*, Jan. 24, 1985, 10.

29. Elliot Abrams, "Diluting Compassion," *New York Times*, Aug. 5, 1983, 19.

30. The Reagan Administration has spent more than $1 billion to prop up the Salvadoran government. See Raymond Bonner, "Sandinistas Aren't the Worst," *New York Times*, Sept. 14, 1984, 29.

31. See generally Lawyers Committee for International Human Rights, *El Salvador's Other Victims: The War on the Displaced* (New York: America's Watch, 1984).

32. One explanation for the callousness of the U.S. government with regard to Salvadorans seeking safety in this country is that this might well involve very large numbers of people, particularly in light of the widespread killing of civilians in that country. Timothy King has argued that the rationale for admitting one individual to another nation could often be used to admit a very large number of individuals. See Timothy King, "Immigration from Developing Countries: Some Philosophical Issues," *Ethics* 93 (1983): 525–36. A recent U.S. Court of Appeals decision used the same rationale. "If we were to agree with the petitioner's contention that no person should be returned to El Salvador because of the reported anarchy present there now, it would permit the whole population, if they could enter this country some way, to stay here indefinitely. There must be some special circumstances present before relief can be granted." *Martinez-Romero v. INS*, 692 F.2d 595 (9th Cir., 1982). I recognize that my proposition might in fact involve very large numbers of people, but I am not at all convinced that this fact in any way lessens the special obligations that we have incurred. For a further discussion of this point see Chapter 10.

33. Since 1960 the EVD program has been instituted for the nationals of 15 different countries where there was a civil war or severe domestic disturbance in the homeland. This list includes: Cuba (1960–66), Czechoslovakia (1968–present), Chile (April–May 1971), Cambodia (1975–77), Vietnam (1975–77), Laos (1975–77), Lebanon (1976–present), Ethiopia (1971–81; still in effect for those who arrived prior to June 1980), Hungary (1971–present), Rumania (1977–present), Uganda (1978–present), Nicaragua (1979–80), Iran (1979), Afghanistan (1980–present), Poland (1981–present). There are case-by-case determinations at the present time in Czechoslovakia, Hungary, Rumania, Uganda, Nicaragua and Iran. See, T. Alexander Aleinikoff, "Political Asylum in the Federal Republic of Germany and the Republic of France: Lessons for the United States," *University of Michigan Journal of Law Reform* 17 (1984): 239.

34. For a discussion of why Sanctuary is a valid means of civil dis-

obedience see Mark Gibney, "Citizen Involvement in Central America," *Contemporary Review*, May, 1985.

35. One of Jimmy Carter's most palpable political blunders occurred when he initially announced that all Cubans who wanted to come to the United States would be welcomed "with open arms." When it soon became apparent that this nation's ideological affinity was not what the President had originally thought it was, he soon had to interpret this statement in a much different way. See David M. Alpern et al., "Carter and the Cuban Influx," *Newsweek*, May 26, 1980, 27.

36. *Statistical Yearbook of the Immigration and Naturalization Service, 1979*, table 8, p. 18.

37. Ibid.

38. See International Labour Office, *1979 Yearbook of Labour Statistics* (Geneva: International Labour Office, 1979).

39. *Memorandum for Wilford Forbush*, Director of Cuban-Haitian Task Force, from Larry Willets, Director, Data Systems and Analysis, Report of Health and Human Services, March 18, 1981. The class of professionals, technical workers, and managers comprised 3 percent of the Haitian "entrants."

40. See U.S. Cong., Senate, Hearings before the Subcommittee on Immigration and Refugee Policy of the Committee on the Judiciary, *United States as a Country of Mass First Asylum*, 97th Cong., 1st sess., July 31, 1981.

41. See Brian Weinstein and Aaron Segal, *Haiti: Political Failures, Cultural Successes* (New York: Praeger Special Studies, 1984). Weinstein and Segal argue that the U.S. presence in this period helped to push Haiti into a dual society, one part that is quite wealthy, while the other part, the much larger portion of Haitian society, is absolutely destitute. Assuming this is true, the Harm Principle should not be invoked for such nebulous activities, absent extenuating circumstances.

42. One possible means of U.S. harm to certain Haitians is the forcible return of Haitians who have come to the United States illegally, and their subsequent persecution back on the island. The empirical evidence on whether those who are returned to Haiti are in fact singled out for persecution is mixed. The *HRC* case spent considerable time on this issue, Judge King ultimately holding that returnees are subject to persecution for their attempts to emigrate. This finding was in conflict with a special State Department report. What is much clearer is the legal standard that a nation must follow: under the well-established principle of nonrefoulement, a nation is obligated not to return an individual to her country if she would face persecution upon her return.

43. *HRC*, 503 F. Supp. at 452.

44. The analogy for this is usually given in terms of aiding members rather than strangers. For example, Jan Naverson writes, "One reason for doing things for those we know rather than those we don't know, is precisely that we do know them, and thus can be reasonably confident that they really would enjoy certain things and not others, that they wouldn't be embarrassed and so on." *Morality and Utility* (Baltimore: Johns Hopkins University Press, 1967), 252. It should be noted, however, that when we are speaking of subsistence itself there should be very little uncertainty in terms of what individuals need and desperately want—food and shelter.

45. See Samuel Chavkin, *The Murder of Chile* (New York: Everest House, 1981); see also Edward Boorstein, *Allende's Chile* (New York: International Publishers, 1977). For a discussion of one view of U.S. complicity in the practices of unjust regimes throughout the world see Noam Chomsky and Edward Herman, *The Political Economy of Human Rights* (Boston: South End Press, 1979).

46. See Michael Leeden and William Lewis, *Debacle: The American Failure in Iran* (New York: Knopf Press, 1981); see also Rich Ramozani, *The United States and Iran: The Patterns of Influence* (New York: Praeger Press, 1982).

47. 531 F. 2d 155 (3d Cir., 1976).

48. In this regard one might question Israel's activities in Ethiopia. One might well argue that more lives would be saved if economic assistance was given rather than emigration to Israel. In response, as a sovereign nation Israel should have a great deal of leeway in how it meets the basic rights of others.

Chapter 10
Present Policy Compared

Legal migration to the United States has been dominated by two policy goals. In terms of normal flow immigration, family reunification practices have been the mainstay of U.S. policy, especially since 1965, although some have clamored for a greater emphasis on meeting manpower goals. Those coming into this country as lawfully admitted "refugees" have invariably been individuals who are fleeing communist regimes.[1] In this chapter I will explore each of these avenues for admission, and I will compare these rationales for admission with those that underlie the Harm Principle (HP) and the Basic Rights Principle (BRP). In addition, I will look at some of the policy implications of the alien admission system proposed in these pages.

NORMAL FLOW IMMIGRATION

Family reunification has always been an integral part of U.S. alien admission policy, but it was not until the 1965 Immigration Act that it became *the* central feature of our immigration system.[2] Approximately 94 percent of the current normal flow admissions to the United States are based on a family relationship. The ascendancy of the family reunification principle was heralded as a great humanitarian advance, and it was. In a sense this nation has made a policy decision that reuniting families was "more important" than meeting manpower needs. Moreover, the ascendancy of the family reunification principle is a sterling example of the way in which moral concerns play a vital role in a nation's policy objectives.

Meeting Manpower Goals

Although current U.S. alien admission policy is centered around the notion of reuniting families, some scholars and policymakers have argued that this policy will have a detrimental effect on the nation's economy. Perhaps the most articulate proponent of pursuing national manpower goals through an alien admission system is Vernon Briggs.[3] Briggs argues that manpower concerns have never played an important role in U.S. immigration policy even when occupational preferences constituted a much larger portion of our quota system. Despite such unintended consequences, U.S. immigration policy has evolved from a system admitting "huddled masses," to one which is now dominated by those of very high socioeconomic status.[4] Briggs recognizes this upper class slant, but his point is that there has been a change since 1970. The change that concerns Briggs results from a combination of factors: increased legal migration from the Western Hemisphere (where human capital traits have traditionally been lower than for those from the Eastern Hemisphere), increased refugee flows (not dominated in recent years by the wealthy and well educated as in the past), increased illegal migration to the United States (again, dominated by Western Hemisphere countries), and essentially no policy with regard to the economic impact of nonimmigrants, those who enter for limited stays, but who generally have the opportunity to work in this country.

Briggs's point is that given these changes in the socioeconomic backgrounds of aliens recently admitted (legally or illegally), much more attention has to be given to the economic impact, particularly the employment impact, of alien admissions.[5] Briggs's point is well made and well taken. He presents perhaps the clearest example of a "trustee" argument in the context of alien admissions: in admitting aliens the primary concern should be what aliens can give to this nation. Manpower goals are unquestionably important, and they are a very legitimate goal for a nation to pursue through its alien admission system. My position, however, is that the "trustee" argument should not be without a moral component. Under the scheme I propose, manpower goals (or other national goals) should be pursued only after a nation has met its obligations under the HP and the BRP.

Family Reunification

Despite some discussion of meeting manpower goals through our alien admission system, the family reunification principle now seems sacrosanct. Charles Keely defends the principle with this powerful language:

The United States is a pluralistic country. We, as a nation, can not only accept, but are enriched in countless ways, by traditions which honor the family and stress close ties not only within the nuclear family of spouses and children but also among generations and among brothers and sisters. Attacks on family reunification beyond the immediate family as a form of nepotism are empty posturing.[6]

The Final Report of the President's Select Commission on Immigration and Refugee Policy did not challenge the premise of family reunification. In fact, the recommendations of the report advocated some policies that would enlarge the scope of "family" for immigration purposes. For instance, the committee report recommended that the nonquota category be expanded to include adult unmarried sons and daughters and grandparents of adult U.S. citizens. In addition, the Select Commission suggested that the quota category for spouses and unmarried sons and daughters of resident aliens be greatly expanded.

The Select Commission also expressed dissatisfaction with the fact that our present method of reuniting families does not accurately reflect (and seek to reunify) the closest family ties:

Of the more than one million persons now registered at consular offices waiting for visas, more than 700,000 are relatives of U.S. citizens or resident aliens, including spouses and minor children of resident aliens. There is something wrong with a law that keeps out—for as long as eight years—the small child of a mother or father who has settled in the United States while a nonrelative or less close relative from another country can come in immediately.[7]

Family reunification *is* a very positive goal to pursue. Keely indeed expresses a deep-seated conviction that families are quite important to individuals, and that our nation has been strengthened by the recognition of family ties. My position acknowledges the importance of family ties, but it also recognizes that the moral obligations that a nation will have under the HP and the BRP should be met before a nation pursues a policy like family reunification. For one thing, the family separation that prompts family reunification is, in the great number of instances, voluntary. That is, individuals who have left family and country to come to the United States have done so on their own accord. The idea of family reunification in this country should not obscure the fact that family reunification is also possible in other lands, particularly in the homeland that has been left behind.

Some might argue that keeping family members apart would cause harm to those individuals affected (assuming that this nation made family reunification subservient to the HP and the BRP). But, as I have already noted, separation is almost always freely chosen. In addition, even if one could accept that there is some kind of harm that has not been freely chosen, it surely is not the kind of harm that meets the threshold level for HP or BRP purposes—life, limb, and vitality.

The system I propose, then, would maintain a family reunification system, but pursue this goal only after a nation has met its HP and BRP duties, through alien admissions or otherwise. The rationale for family reunification is important, and those who are admitted to this country under either the HP or the BRP should be able to bring close family members with them. This kind of separation from family would not be freely chosen. In specifying close family relatives I might be exhibiting certain Western biases. I recognize this, but there are millions of people in need and we should be looking at the very serious cases of need. Some lines have to be drawn, and I would draw them at close family members.

REFUGEE ADMISSIONS

The other major avenue of legal migration to the United States occurs through refugee admission. For a large part of American history no special provisions were made for those suffering from persecution in their homeland.[8] After World War II legislative action was taken so that those who particularly suffered from the war were given special preference in admission to this country.[9] During the 1950s and early 1960s the Attorney General frequently used his statutory parole power to admit individuals who were thought to be suffering persecution in the home country.[10] Invariably these individuals came from communist countries.

In 1965 a new seventh preference was added to the Immigration Act which was intended to institute a procedure to admit refugees from the Middle East and communist countries.[11] Despite this new provision, most of those coming to this country as "refugees" continued to do so under the Attorney General's parole power.[12] In 1980 the Refugee Act was passed, abandoning previous ideological and geographical restrictions, and making another effort to harness the Attorney General's power.[13] It is questionable how effective the Refugee Act has been in achieving its purpose. The Cuban "entrants" admitted to the United States immediately after passage of the Refugee Act were admitted under the Attorney General's actions. In addition, as we have already noted, refugee and asylum relief still has a definite flavor of the East-West conflict.[14]

My position with regard to admission from communist regimes is quite similar to that taken in the last section with regard to family reunification, and meeting national manpower goals. I commend the practice of admitting individuals from communist regimes because these societies truly do seem unjust by virtually any standard. However, we should pursue such activities only after we have met our HP and BRP obligations. It should be noted that if those living in communist nations are in serious need, then assistance to these individuals could be premised on the BRP (I am assuming we have not helped to perpetuate these regimes and therefore caused harm to the population under the HP). This is also to say, however, that merely living in a communist regime should not be equated with meeting BRP criteria; nor can it be said that all, or nearly all, of those who have been admitted to this country as refugees from communist countries have been persecuted in their homeland. The empirical evidence argues against this quite convincingly.

Robert Bach has shown that economic considerations have been at least as important as political motivations for each wave of Cuban migrants coming to this country.[15] There has also been a good deal of concern whether many of those leaving Vietnam the past few years are merely following economic motives.[16] I do not mean to totally disparage economic motivations—after all this factor seems dominant in normal flow admissions as well—however, we do need to separate stereotype from reality. Finally, data collected by Rita Simon seems to raise the question whether those currently coming to this country as refugees are in as much need as those whom we would admit/aid under the HP and the BRP.[17]

It might be argued that our affinity to other groups is being ignored under the system I am trying to establish. I argued in Chapter 1 that I am not sure we can easily speak of just a few affinities in a pluralist society like the United States. I am willing to admit that there does seem to be a widespread affinity with those attempting to leave communist countries (although the empirical data also shows that the American public does not seem particularly pleased with resettlement in this country). But is is also likely that in recognizing this particular affinity we are, at the same time, ignoring a whole host of other affinities that exist in this society. Sanctuary seems to offer such a counterexample. Even if we felt quite secure that we have in fact recognized all possible affinities (and why shouldn't all affinities be recognized?), I would still argue that we should only satisfy such affinities *after* our duties under the HP and the BRP have been met. In other words, in comparing obligations and affinities we should first honor our obligations to others.

POLICY IMPLICATIONS OF THE PROPOSED SYSTEM

The last item to be addressed is the policy implications of the alien admission system proposed here. It is important to note how the proposed system differs, but at the same time reflects, past and present U.S. alien admissions. The differences are undoubtedly more striking. Current normal flow immigration is based on reuniting families, while the proposed system seeks to meet the basic rights of individuals, particularly those we have harmed. In other respects, however, the humanitarian aspects of the proposed system are quite similar to the humanitarianism that is ostensibly the basis for both refugee and normal flow admissions. My point is that the humanitarianism in the proposed system is a deeper level of humanitarianism that what is met under current policy. It is a humanitarianism based on obligations to individuals in serious need; the present system is not. As a policy consequence, the types of people who would gain admission under the proposed system will undoubtedly be much different in kind than those currently being admitted. The reader will recall that one of my criticisms of both normal flow and refugee admissions is that those admitted are quite atypical of the sending societies. Again, my concern is that a purportedly humanitarian program has ignored those in serious need.

In addition to admitting different types of people, which might bring disruptions to U.S. society not experienced under current policy, the proposed system could bring political, economic, and social disruptions by the numbers of individuals admitted. The reader will recall that one of the arguments made is that if a nation has caused (or very well might cause) severe harm to individuals in another society (and if restitution cannot be made in other ways) this will obligate very large-scale alien admissions to the nation causing harm (although there is no obligation of permanent settlement).

Does the proposed system ignore the ability of a nation to absorb aliens? No it does not. The proposed system has clearly recognized the disruption to a community that alien admissions can bring. Admission under the BRP, and any admission of aliens in the pursuit of "national" goals (such as manpower goals or family reunification), needs to be quite sensitive to the absorptive capacities of a country. However, I find a concern for minimizing societal disruption much less compelling when we are speaking of a situation where individuals in other societies have been harmed by the actions of another nation. It is essential to realize that the large-scale alien admissions that might be dictated under the HP only occurs *because* one nation has caused harm to individuals in another society. That is, without this initial act of causing harm to others, no widespread alien admission is warranted. As comments in this chapter by Briggs and Keely indicate, the "trustee" argument can take many forms and guises. To be clear, I am not against the pursuit of such national goals and concerns. However, they have their proper place, and their proper place is after a nation has met its deeper obligations under the HP and the BRP.

CONCLUSION

I have done several things in this chapter. The first was to examine other rationales for admitting individuals to this country. I have focused on the two main policy goals this country has at present: reuniting families, and admitting individuals who live under totalitarian regimes. Both goals are quite commendable. My point in this chapter, however, is that these goals should only be pursued after we have met our obligations under the HP and the BRP.

The second purpose of this chapter relates to the first. I have tried to show how we must separate stereotype from reality. In terms of the family reunification principle, I have shown how most individuals freely choose the initial separation from their family. In addition, I have argued that the separation of families does not speak to the same kinds of harms that are addressed by the HP and the BRP, if in fact we are speaking of harm here at all. In terms of admission from communist countries, I have shown that many of those coming to this country under this policy are often moved by considerations other than persecution for certain beliefs, and that the need of many of those coming from communist countries would not reach the same levels as that experienced by those we would help under the HP and the

BRP. My final point was to examine the implications of the proposed system. This system is not meant as an "ideal" theory, although the dominance of the "trustee" view, in its present form at least, might tend to make it seem as such.

NOTES

1. It should also be pointed out that family reunification has played an integral role in refugee relief as well. Preference categories for "Displaced Persons" reflected family connections (as well as U.S. manpower needs). At the present time it is estimated that 80 percent of the refugees we admit from Southeast Asia have a family connection with this country. See Robert Wright, "Voluntary Agencies and the Resettlement of Refugees," *International Migration Review* 15 (1980): 157–74.

2. For example, compare the preference system in the 1952 Immigration Act with that in the 1965 Act. In the 1952 Act (and before) occupation preferences were always at least 50 percent of the first preference. Moreover, the definition of "family" was much narrower in the 1952 Act than it was under the 1965 Act. See E. P. Hutchinson, *Legislative History of American Immigration Policy 1798–1965* (Philadelphia: University of Pennsylvania Press, 1981).

3. Vernon Briggs, Jr., *Immigration Policy and the American Labor Force* (Baltimore: Johns Hopkins University Press, 1984).

4. An examination of how the socioeconomic backgrounds of immigrants have drastically changed is quite revealing. For example, in 1910, 1.2 percent of the aliens admitted to this country (all of this data is for those who declared an occupation at the time of entry) were professional and technical workers, compared with 4.7 percent of the U.S. work force. By 1930 the socioeconomic status for aliens pretty much reflected the American work force, at least for this high socioeconomic group, with 6.3 percent of the aliens in this category as compared with 6.8 percent of the U.S. work force. In 1950 16.2 percent of the aliens, but only 8.6 percent of the American work force, fell into the professional and technical worker category. In 1960 the comparisons were 17.9 percent and 11.2 percent. In 1970 29.4 percent of the aliens admitted to the United States were in this socioeconomic category compared with only 14.2 percent of the American work force. See David North and William Weissert, *Immigrants and the American Labor Market*, Manpower Administration Research Monograph No. 31 (Washington, D.C.: U.S. Dept. of Labor, 1974), 92–93. My point, quite simply, is that this type of alien admissions is a far cry from the "huddled masses" this nation would like to believe it admits.

5. Briggs is a firm believer in the idea that aliens will often displace U.S. workers from certain jobs. See his article "Foreign Labor Programs as an Alternative to Illegal Migration: A Dissenting View," in Peter Brown and Henry Shue, eds., *The Border That Joins: Mexican Migrants and U.S. Responsibility* (Totowa, N.J.: Rowman and Littlefield, 1983). For the opposite conclusion see Edwin Reubens, "Immigration Problems, Limited-Visa Programs, and Other Options," in that same volume.

6. Charles Keely, "Family Reunification," *U.S. Immigration Policy and the National Interest, Staff Report of the Select Commission on Immigration and Refugee Policy*, appendix D, p. 48.

7. *U.S. Immigration Policy and the National Interest, Final Report and Recommendations of the Select Commission on Immigration and Refugee Policy*, p. 14.

8. For a good discussion of the history of U.S. policy in this area see Harry Francis Mullaly, "United States Refugee Policy 1789–1956" (thesis, New York University, 1960).

9. Displaced Persons Act of 1948, ch 647 62 Stat. 1009 as amended by Act of June 16, 1950, ch 262, 64 Stat. 219; Act of June 28, 1951, ch 167, 65 Stat. 96 (repealed 1957). Some have argued that our policy of aiding those harmed by the war was not as altruistic as it was portrayed. For an argument that these programs were designed to avoid having to admit Jews who had been in concentration camps see Leonard Dinnerstein, *America and the Survivors of the Holocaust* (New York: Columbia University Press, 1982).

10. It has to be noted, however, that not all of those suffering persecution, or apparently suffering persecution, were welcomed to this country. John Scanlan and Gilburt Loescher have pointed out that in the first wave of Cubans, draft age men were excluded from migrating to the United States. See "U.S. Foreign Policy, 1959–1980: Impact on Refugee Flow From Cuba," *The Annals of the American Academy of Political and Social Sciences*, special ed. Gilburt Loescher and John Scanlan (Beverly Hills: Sage, 1983).

11. Immigration and Nationality Act, Publ. L. 89–236, 79 Stat. 911 (1965).

12. Arthur Helton has broken down admission under the Attorney General's parole power into two time frames. For pre–1968 admissions, 925 individuals from noncommunist nations and 232,711 individuals from communist nations were paroled into this country. During the period 1968–80, 7,150 individuals from noncommunist nations were paroled into the United States compared with 608,365 individuals from communist nations. See Arthur Helton, "Political Asylum Under the

1980 Refugee Act," *University of Michigan Journal of Law Reform* 17 (1984): 243, 246–48. See also Sen. Rept. No. 256, 96th Cong. 1st sess., 6, reprinted in 1980 *U.S. Code Congressional and Admin. News* 141, 146 (Historical Summary of Refugee Parole Action).

13. Refugee Act of 1980, Pub. L. 96–212, March 17, 1980 94 Stat. 109 (1980).

14. For a good discussion of how the bureaucratic machinery operates today much like it did before passage of the Refugee Act see Michael Posner and Susan Kaplan, "Who Should We Let In?" *Human Rights* (Summer, 1981).

15. Robert Bach, "The New Cuban Immigrants: Their Backgrounds and Prospects," *Monthly Labor Review* 103 (1980): 39–46.

16. U.S. Cong., House, Committee on the Judiciary, *Refugee Issues in Southeast Asia and Europe and International Issues on Drug Enforcement and Administrative Law*, 97th Cong., 2nd sess. (1982).

17. For example, when Russian fathers were asked reasons for leaving the Soviet Union, the following responses were given: anti-Semitism—13 percent; lack of opportunity for respondent—6 percent; lack of opportunity for children—22 percent; combination of anti-Semitism and lack of opportunity—46 percent; lack of freedom—7 percent. When asked the same sort of question, fathers from Vietnam responded in the following fashion: live in a free society, oppose communist regime—68 percent; worked with U.S. forces or South Vietnamese government and fearful of life—20 percent; job and educational opportunities under the new regime—6 percent; join family member already in the U.S.—6 percent. See Rita Simon, "Russian and Vietnamese Immigrant Families: A Comparative Analysis of Parental and Adolescent's Adjustments to Their New Society," *U.S. Immigration Policy and the National Interest, Staff Report of the Select Commission on Immigration and Refugee Policy*, appendix C.

Concluding Remarks

Concerns about alien admission practices will continue to grow in the United States. The cry that we have lost control of our national borders is nothing new to our history. Demographic patterns in developing countries will only heighten what seems to be an intractable problem today. This work was largely inspired by a belief that some of the most vital questions concerning alien admission practices have been ignored in the current debate on immigration policy. The status quo is family reunification, a much smaller (and shrinking) refugee admission system that is heavily biased toward admitting those from communist regimes, and a perceived problem of too many illegal aliens crossing the nation's southern border. The current debate, I have implicitly argued in these pages, does not challenge any of the underlying assumptions of our alien admission practices. Instead, its focus has been on the problem of illegal aliens and how we should handle this situation, or more accurately, how we can exclude these individuals.

Once particular alien admission practices are established they are quite slow to change or die a natural death. We can now scorn the racist alien admission policies of the past, but it is important to note that this past is not so far removed from us today. The 1965 Immigration Act was indeed a decided advance over the national origins quota system that it replaced. The 1980 Refugee Act was also an advance over a system that seemed to pay little heed to the needs of individuals in other countries. It is my belief, however, that it is possible to frame and implement an even better alien admission system than the one this nation has at the present time. It is this challenge that I have attempted to meet. Such a system would recognize the need to maintain the communal processes in this country; but it would also devote far more effort to meet the basic rights of individuals in other lands, particularly those whose plight we are responsible for. Alien admissions should be used to protect communities, but it should also be used to protect individuals as well.

Selected Bibliography

Ackerman, Bruce. *Social Justice in the Liberal State*. New Haven: Yale University Press, 1980.
Aleinikoff, T. Alexander. "Aliens, Due Process and Community Ties: A Response to Martin." *University of Pittsburgh Law Review* 44 (1983): 237–260.
———. "Political Asylum in the Federal Republic of Germany and the Republic of France: Lessons for the United States." *University of Michigan Journal of Law Reform* 17 (1984): 183–241.
Aleinikoff, T. Alexander, and David Martin. *Immigration: Process and Policy*. St. Paul: West Publishing Co., 1985.
Anscombe, Elizabeth. "War and Murder." In *War and Morality*, edited by Richard Wasserstrom, 42–53. Belmont, Calif.: Wadsworth Press, 1970.
"Any Place But Here: A Critique of United States Hazardous Export Policy." *Brooklyn Journal of International Law* 7 (1982): 329–63.
Bach, Robert. "The New Cuban Immigrants: Their Background and Prospects." *Monthly Labor Review* 103 (1980): 39–46.
Baker, Ernest. *Social Contracts: Essays by Locke, Hume, and Rousseau*. New York: Oxford University Press, 1962.
Baldwin, David. "Foreign Aid, Intervention, and Influence." *World Politics* 21 (1964): 425–37.
Barry, Brian. *The Liberal Theory of Justice*. Oxford: Clarendon Press, 1973.

———. *Rich Countries and Poor Countries.* (unpublished manuscript, copy with author).
Beitz, Charles. *Political Theory and International Relations.* Princeton: Princeton University Press, 1979.
———. "Bounded Morality: Justice and the State in World Politics." *International Organization* 33 (1979): 405–24.
Boorstein, Edward. *Allende's Chile.* New York: International Publishers, 1977.
Briggs, Vernon, Jr. "Foreign Labor Programs as an Alternative to Illegal Migration: A Dissenting View." In *The Border That Joins: Mexican Migrants and U.S. Responsibility,* edited by Peter Brown and Henry Shue, 223–45. Totowa, N.J.: Rowman and Littlefield, 1983.
———. *Immigration Policy and the American Labor Force.* Baltimore: Johns Hopkins University Press, 1984.
Brown, Peter. "Food as National Property." In *Food Policy: The Responsibility of the United States in the Life and Death Choices,* edited by Peter Brown and Henry Shue, 65–78. New York: Free Press, 1977.
Bull, Hedley. *The Anarchical Society: A Study of Order in World Politics.* New York: Columbia University Press, 1977.
Campbell, T. D. "Humanity Before Justice." *British Journal of Political Science* 4 (1974); 1–16.
Chaney, Elsa. "Migrant Workers and National Boundaries: The Basis for Rights and Protections." In *Boundaries: National Autonomy and Its Limits,* edited by Peter Brown and Henry Shue, 37–77. Totowa, N.J.: Rowman and Littlefield, 1981.
Chavkin, Samuel. *The Murder of Chile.* New York: Everest House, 1981.
Chomsky, Noam, and Edward Herman. *The Washington Connection and Third World Fascism: The Political Economy of Human Rights.* Boston: South End Press, 1979.
Cohen, Marshall. "Moral Skepticism and International Relations." *Philosophy and Public Affairs* 13 (1984), 299–346.
Cong. Rec. December 12, 1982, H.10123–10168.
Cong. Rec. September 5, 1980, E.4232.
Cong. Rec. March 24, 1981, S.2579–2583.
Convention Governing the Specific Aspects of Refugee Problems in Africa. U.N.T.S. no. 14691, (1964).
Convention Relative to the Protection of Civilian Persons in War. 6 U.S.T., 3516 T.I.A.S., 75 U.N.T.S. (1949).
Cornelius, Wayne. "Illegal Migration to the United States: Recent Research Findings and Policy Implications." *Selected Readings on U.S. Immigration Policy and the Law,* 67–76. Washington, D.C.: GPO, 1980.

Crewdson, John. *The Tarnished Door: The New Immigrants and the Transformation of America.* New York: Times Books, 1983.
Dinnerstein, Leonard. *America and the Survivors of the Holocaust.* New York: Columbia University Press, 1982.
Dixon, David. "Thatcher's People: The British Nationality Act of 1981." *Journal of Law and Society* 10 (1983): 161–80.
Doppelt, Gerald. "Statism Without Foundations." *Philosophy and Public Affairs* 9 (1975): 398–403.
Falk, Richard. *The Role of Domestic Courts in the International Legal Order.* Syracuse: Syracuse University Press, 1964.
Feinberg, Joel. *Rights, Justice and the Bounds of Justice.* Princeton: Princeton University Press, 1980.
Ferencz, Benjamin. *Less Than Slaves.* Cambridge: Harvard University Press, 1979.
Fishkin, James. *The Limits of Obligation.* New Haven: Yale University Press, 1982.
Forbes, Susan. "The Half Open Door: Illegal Migration to the United States." *U.S. Immigration Policy and the National Interest. Staff Report of the Select Commission on Immigration and Refugee Policy.* 457–558. Washington, D.C.: GPO, 1981.
Fried, Charles. *An Anatomy of Values: Problems of Personal and Social Choice.* Cambridge: Harvard University Press, 1970.
Friedrich, Carl. "The Concept of Community in the History of Political and Legal Philosophy." *Nomos II* (Community), 3–24. New York: Liberal Arts Press, 1959.
Fullinwider, Robert. "War and Innocence." *Philosophy and Public Affairs* 5 (1975): 90–97.
Gallup Opinion Index. Princeton: American Institute of Public Opinion, May 1975, 2.
Gallup Opinion Index. Princeton: American Institute of Public Opinion, September 1979, 8–11.
Geneva Convention Relating to the Status of Refugees. 19 U.S.T. 6260, T.I.A.S. 6377 (1951).
Ghoshal, Animesh. "Political Versus Economic Refugees." *U.S. Immigration Policy and the National Interest. Staff Report of the Select Commission on Immigration and Refugee Policy,* appendix C, 209–26. Washington, D.C.: GPO, 1981.
Gibney, Mark. "Seeking Sanctuary: A Special Duty for the U.S.?" *Commonweal,* May 18, 1984, 295–96.
———. "Citizen Involvement in Central America." *Contemporary Review,* May 1985, 225–29.
———. "The Role of the Judiciary In Alien Admissions." *Boston College International and Comparative Law Review* 8 (1985): 341–76.

Goodwin-Gill, Guy. *The Refugee in International Law.* Oxford: Clarendon Press, 1983.
Gordon, C., and H. Rosenfeld. *Immigration Law and Procedure.* New York: Matthew Bender, 1984.
Gough, J. W. *The Social Contract.* 2d ed. Oxford: Clarendon Press, 1957.
Grahl-Madsen, Atle. "Refugees and Refugee Law in a World of Transition." *Transnational Legal Problems of Refugees, 1982 Michigan Yearbook of International Legal Studies,* 65–88. New York: Clark Boardman Company, Ltd.
Grassmuck, George. (unpublished manuscript on voting behavior in the U.S. Congress on immigration legislation in the 1920s, copy with author).
Hardin, Garrett. "Lifeboat Ethics: The Case Against Helping the Poor." In *World Hunger and Moral Obligation,* edited by William Aiken and Hugh LaFollette, 11–21. Englewood Cliffs, N.J.: Prentice Hall, 1977.
Hare, R. M. "Rawls' Theory of Justice." In *Reading Rawls,* edited by Norm Daniels, 81–107. New York: Basic Books, 1975.
Hart, H. L. A. "Are There Any Natural Rights?" *Philosophical Review* 64 (1955): 175–91.
Helton, Arthur C. "Political Asylum Under the 1980 Refugee Act: An Unfulfilled Promise." *University of Michigan Journal of Law Reform* 17 (1984): 243–64.
Higham, John. *Strangers in the Land.* New York: Atheneum Press, 1960.
Hoffman, Stanley. *Duties Beyond Borders: On the Limits and Possibilities of Ethical International Politics.* Syracuse: Syracuse University Press, 1981.
Hofstetter, Richard. "Economic Underdevelopment and the Population Explosion: Implications for U.S. Immigration Policy." *Law and Contemporary Problems* 45 (1982): 55–79.
Huntington, Samuel. "Foreign Aid For What and For Whom?" In *Development Today,* edited by Robert Hunter and John Reilly, 21–60. New York: Praeger, 1972.
Hutchinson, E. P. *Legislative History of American Immigration Policy 1798–1965.* Philadelphia: University of Pennsylvania Press, 1981.
"Immigration Policy and the Rights of Aliens." *Harvard Law Review* 96 (1983): 1286–1465.
International Labour Office. *1979 Yearbook of Labour Statistics.* Geneva: International Labour Office, 1979.
Isaacs, Arnold. *Without Honor: Defeat in Vietnam and Cambodia.* Baltimore: John Hopkins University Press, 1983.
James, Susan. "The Duty to Relieve Suffering." *Ethics* 93 (1982): 4–21.
Kalumiya, Kallu. *Re: UNHCR Mandate Definition of Refugee and the Sit-*

uation of Salvadoran Asylum Seekers. Washington, D.C., Office of Legal Counsel, United Nations. February 1982 (copy with author).

Karst, Kenneth. "Equality and Community: Lessons from the Civil Rights Era." *Notre Dame Lawyer* 56 (1981): 179–214.

Keely, Charles. "Effects of U.S. Immigration Law on Manpower Characteristics." *Demography* 12 (1975): 179–91.

———. "Family Reunification."*U.S. Immigration Policy and the National Interest. Staff Report of the Select Commission on Immigration and Refugee Policy*, appendix D, 47–54. Washington, D.C.: GPO, 1981.

———. *Global Refugee Policy: The Case for a Development-Oriented Strategy.* New York: Population Council, 1981.

Kelly, Gail Paradise. *From Vietnam to America.* Boulder: Westview Press, 1977.

King, Timothy. "Immigration from Developing Countries: Some Philosophical Issues." *Ethics* 93 (1983): 526–36.

Kirkpatrick, Jeanne. "Dictatorships and Double Standards." In *Human Rights and U.S. Human Rights Policy*, edited by Howard J. Wiarda, 5–29. Washington, D.C.: American Enterprise Institute, 1982.

Lawrence, Daniel. *Black Migrants: White Natives; A Study of Race Relations in Nottingham.* Cambridge: Cambridge University Press, 1974.

Lawyers Committee for International Human Rights. *El Salvador's Other Victims: The War on the Displaced.* New York: America's Watch, April 1984.

Leeden, Michael, and William Lewis. *Debacle: The American Failure in Iran.* New York: Knopf Press, 1981.

Lichtenberg, Judith. "Mexican Migration and U.S. Policy: A Guide for the Perplexed." In *The Border That Joins: Mexican Migrants and U.S. Responsibility*, edited by Peter Brown and Henry Shue, 13–30. Totowa, N.J.: Rowman and Littlefield, 1983.

Liu, William. *Transition to Nowhere.* Nashville: Charter House Publisher, 1979.

Lopez, Gerald. "Undocumented Mexican Migration: In Search of a Just Immigration Law and Policy."*U.C.L.A. Law Review* 28 (1983): 615–714.

MacLean, Douglas. "Constraints, Goals, and Moralism in Foreign Policy." In *Human Rights and U.S. Foreign Policy*, edited by Peter Brown and Douglas MacLean, 93–108. Lexington, Mass.: Lexington Books, 1979.

Martin, David. "The Refugee Act of 1980: Its Past and Future: *Transnational Legal Problems of Refugees, 1982 Michigan Yearbook of International Legal Studies*, 91–123. New York: Clark Boardman Company, Ltd.

———. "Due Process and the Treatment of Aliens." *University of Pittsburgh Law Review* 44 (1983): 165–235.
Mavrodes, George. "Conventions and the Morality of War." *Philosophy and Public Affairs* 4 (1975): 117–31.
Melden, A. I. *Rights and Persons*. Berkeley: University of California Press, 1977.
Miller, David. *Social Justice*. Oxford: Oxford University Press, 1976.
Morris, Milton. *Immigration—The Beleagured Bureaucracy*. Washington, D.C.: Brookings Institute, 1985.
Mullaly, Harry Francis. "United States Refugee Policy 1789–1956." Thesis, New York University, 1960.
Muller, Ronald, and Richard Barnett. *Global Reach: The Power of the Multinational Corporations*. New York: Simon and Schuster, 1979.
Mutharika, Peter. *The Alien Under American Law*. New York: Ocean Pub., 1981.
Nagel, Thomas. "Ruthlessness in Public Life." In *Public and Private Morality*, edited by Stuart Hampshire, 75–91. Cambridge: Cambridge University Press, 1978.
Nardin, Terry. *Law, Morality, and the Relations of States*. Princeton: Princeton University Press, 1983.
Naverson, Jan. *Morality and Utility*. Baltimore: Johns Hopkins University Press, 1967.
North, David, and William Weissert. *Immigrants and the American Labor Market*. Manpower Administration Research Monograph No. 31. Washington, D.C.: U.S. Department of Labor, 1974.
North, David, and Marion Houstoun. "The Characteristics and Role of Illegal Aliens in the U.S. Labor Market." *Selected Readings on U.S. Immigration Policy and Law*, 77–98. Washington, D.C.: GPO, 1980.
Patterson, Sheila. *Immigration and Race Relations in Britain 1960–1967*. Oxford: Oxford University Press, 1969.
Pido, Antonio. "Brain Drain Philippines." *Society* 14 (1977): 50–53.
Piore, Michael. *Birds of Passage: Migrant Labor and Industrial Society*. New York: Cambridge University Press, 1980.
Pitkin, Hannah. "Obligations and Consent I." *American Political Science Review* 59 (1965): 990–99.
Posner, Michael, and Susan Kaplan. "Who Should We Let In?" *Human Rights*, Summer 1981.
Power, Jonathon. *Migrant Workers in Western Europe and the United States*. Oxford: Pergamon Press, 1979.
Prosser, William. *Handbook of the Law of Torts*. St. Paul: West Publishing Co., 1971.
Ramozani, Rich. *The United States and Iran: The Patterns of Influence*. New York: Praeger Press, 1982.

Rawls, John. *A Theory of Justice*. Cambridge: Harvard University Press, 1971.
Reubens, Edwin. "Immigration Problems, Limited-Visa Programs, and Other Options." In *The Border That Joins: Mexican Migrants and U.S. Responsibility*, edited by Peter Brown and Henry Shue, 187–222. Totowa, N.J.: Rowman and Littlefield, 1983.
Rosberg, Gerald. "'Aliens and Equal Protection: Why Not the Right to Vote?" *University of Michigan Law Review* 77 (1977): 1092–1136.
Scanlan, John. "Immigration Law and the Illusion of Numerical Control." *University of Miami Law Review* 36 (1982): 819–64.
Scanlan, John, and Gilburt Loescher. "U.S. Foreign Policy, 1959–1980: Impact on Refugee Flow From Cuba." In *The Annals of the American Academy of Political and Social Sciences*, 116–37. Special Ed. Gilburt Loescher and John Scanlan. Beverly Hills: Sage, 1983.
Scanlon, Tim. "Rawls' Theory of Justice." In *Reading Rawls*, edited by Norm Daniels, 167–205. New York: Basic Books, 1975.
Schuck, Peter. "The Transformation of Immigration Law." *Columbia Law Review* 84 (1984): 1–90.
Shacknove, Andrew. "Who Is a Refugee?" *Ethics* 95 (1985): 274–84.
Shawcross, William. *Sideshow: Kissinger, Nixon and the Destruction of Cambodia*. New York: Pocket Books, 1979.
Shue, Henry. *Basic Rights: Subsistence, Affluence, and U.S. Foreign Policy*. Princeton: Princeton University Press, 1980.
———. "Exporting Hazards." *Ethics* 91 (1981): 579–606.
Sidgwick, Henry. *The Elements of Politics*. London: Macmillan and Company, 1919.
Simon, Rita. "Russian and Vietnamese Immigrant Families: A Comparative Analysis of Parental and Adolescent's Adjustments to Their New Society." *U.S. Immigration Policy and the National Interest. Staff Report of the Select Commission on Immigration and Refugee Policy*, appendix C, 289–354. Washington, D.C.: GPO, 1981.
Singer, Peter. "Famine, Affluence, and Morality." *Philosophy and Public Affairs* 1 (1972): 229–43.
———. *Animal Liberation*. New York: New York Review, 1975.
———. "Ends and Means." *Practical Ethics*, 182–200. Cambridge: Cambridge University Press, 1979.
Slater, Jerome, and Terry Nardin. "Nonintervention and International Morality." (unpublished paper, copy with author).
Steiner, Hillel. "The Natural Right to the Means of Production." *Philosophical Quarterly* 27 (1977): 41–49.
Stevens, Rosemary, Louis Wolf Goodman, and Stephen S. Mick. *The Alien Doctors*. New York: Wiley Publishers, 1978.
Suhrke, Astri. "Indochinese Refugees: The Law and Politics of Asy-

lum." In *The Annals of the American Academy of Political and Social Sciences* 102–15. Special Ed. Gilburt Loescher and John Scanlan. Beverly Hills: Sage, 1983.

Teitelbaum, Michael. "Right Versus Right: Immigration and Refugee Policy in the United States." *Foreign Affairs* 59 (1980): 21–59.

———. "Immigration, Refugees, and Foreign Policy." *International Organization* 38 (1984): 429–50.

Tienda, Marta. "Familism and Structural Assimilation of Mexican Immigrants." *International Migration Review* 14 (1980): 383–408.

Tucker, Robert. *The Inequality of Nations*. Colorado Springs: Research Committee, 1977.

United Nations. *Reverse Transfer of Technology: A Survey of Its Main Features, Causes, and Policy Implications*. U.N. Conference on Trade and Development. New York: United Nations, 1979.

United Nations. *United Nations High Commissioner for Refugees, Mission to Monitor INS Asylum Processing of Salvadoran Illegal Entrants*. Printed in *Cong. Rec.* S.827–831, February 11, 1982.

U.S. Code Congressional and Administrative News 1980. Washington, D.C.: GPO, 1980, 141–53.

U.S. Cong., House. *Hearings on Immigration*. 97th Cong., 1st sess., Washington, D.C.: GPO, 1981.

U.S. Cong., House. *Refugee Act of 1980 Amendment*. 97th Cong., 1st sess., Washington, D.C.: GPO, 1981.

U.S. Cong., House. *Refugee Issues in Southeast Asia and Europe and International Issues on Drug Enforcement and Administrative Law*. 97th Cong., 2d sess., Washington, D.C.: GPO, 1982.

U.S. Cong., House. *Immigration Reform and Control Act of 1983*. 98th Cong., 2d sess., (H. 1510), printed in *Cong. Rec.* H.6149–6166.

U.S. Cong., House. *Refugee Assistance*. 98th Cong., 1st sess., Washington, D.C.: GPO, 1983.

U.S. Cong., House. *Immigration Reform and Control Act of 1985*. 99th Cong., 1st sess., (H.R. 3080), Washington, D.C.: GPO, 1985.

U.S. Cong., Senate. *Review of U.S. Resettlement Programs and Policies*. 96th Cong., 2d sess., Washington, D.C.: GPO, 1980.

U.S. Cong., Senate. *United States as a Country of Mass First Asylum*. 97th Cong., 1st sess., Washington, D.C.: GPO, 1981.

U.S. Cong., Senate. *Immigration Reform and Control*. 97th Cong., 2d sess., (S. Rept. 485), Washington, D.C.: GPO, 1982.

U.S. Cong., Senate. *Immigration Reform and Control Act of 1983*. 98th Cong., 1st sess., (S. 529), printed in *Cong. Rec.* May 18, 1983, S. 6970–6986.

U.S. Cong., Senate. *Immigration Reform and Control Act of 1985*. 99th Cong., 1st sess., (S. 1200), printed in *Cong. Rec.* September 19, 1985, S. 11750– 11769.

U.S. Dept. of Health and Human Services. Report to the Congress. *Refugee Resettlement Program 1985.* Washington, D.C.: GPO, 1985.

U.S. Dept. of Health and Human Services. *Memorandum for Wilford Forbush*, Director of Cuban/Haitian Task Force, from Larry Willets, Director Data Systems and Analysis. Report of Health and Human Services. March 18, 1981.

U.S. Dept. of Health and Human Services. Report to the Congress. *Refugee Resettlement Program 1981.* Washington, D.C.: GPO, 1981.

U.S. Dept. of Health and Human Services. Report to the Congress. *Refugee Resettlement Program 1982.* Washington, D.C.: GPO, 1982.

U.S. Dept. of Health and Human Services. Report to the Congress. *Refugee Resettlement Program 1983.* Washington, D.C.: GPO, 1983.

U.S. Dept. of Health and Human Services. Report to the Congress. *Refugee Resettlement Program 1984.* Washington, D.C.: GPO, 1984.

U.S. Dept. of Health and Human Services. Report to the Congress. *Refugee Resettlement Program 1985.* Washington, D.C.: GPO, 1985.

U.S. Dept. of Justice. *Statistical Yearbook of the Immigration and Naturalization Service,* 1979. Washington, D.C.: GPO, 1979.

U.S. Departments of Justice, Labor, and State. U.S. Interagency Task Force on Immigration Policy. *Staff Report.* Washington, D.C.: GPO, 1979.

Walzer, Michael. *Obligations: Essays on Civil Disobedience, War, and Citizenship.* Cambridge: Harvard University Press, 1970.

———. *Just and Unjust Wars.* New York: Basic Books, 1977.

———. "The Moral Standing of States: A Response to Four Critics." *Philosophy and Public Affairs* 9 (1980): 209–29.

———. "The Distribution of Membership." In *Boundaries: National Autonomy and Its Limits,* edited by Peter Brown and Henry Shue, 1–35. Totowa, N.J.: Rowman and Littlefield, 1981.

———. *Spheres of Justice.* New York: Basic Books, 1983.

Wasserstrom, Richard. "On the Morality of War: A Preliminary Inquiry." *War and Morality* 78–101. Belmont, Calif.: Wadsworth Press, 1970.

Weinstein, Brian, and Aaron Segal. *Haiti: Political Failures, Cultural Successes.* New York: Praeger Special Studies, 1984.

Weintraub, Sidney. "Illegal Immigration and U.S. Foreign Economic Policy." In *The Unavoidable Issue: U.S. Immigration Policy in the 1980's,* edited by Demetrious Papademetriou and Mark Miller, 215–49. Philadelphia: Institute for the Study of Human Issues, 1983.

Whelen, Frederick. "Citizenship and the Right to Leave." *American Political Science Review* 75 (1981): 636–53.

Wicclair, Mark. "Human Rights and Intervention: A Contractual Analysis." In *John Rawls' Theory of Social Justice: An Introduction*, edited by H. Gene Blocker and Elizabeth H. Smith, 284–308. Athens Ohio: Ohio University Press, 1980.

Wright, Robert. "Voluntary Agencies and the Resettlement of Refugees." *International Migration Review* 15 (1980): 157–74.

Young, Stephen B. "The Legality of Vietnamese Education Camps." *Harvard International Law Journal* 20 (1979): 519–38.

———. "Between Sovereigns: A Re-examination of the Refugee's Status." *Transnational Legal Problems of Refugees, 1982 Michigan Yearbook of International Legal Studies*, 339–70. New York: Clark Boardman Company, Ltd.

Index

Abrams, Elliot, 119
Ackerman, Bruce: on alien dialogues, 47–50, 97; basis for admitting aliens, 47–49, 51–52, 54 n.8; on East-West dialogue, 48–49, 51–52; on foreign assistance, 52–53; on liberal dialogue, 48–49, 50–51, 53; on liberal state, 50–53, 54 n.11; on "Z" cutoff for admissions, 48, 51–52, 54 n.8, 108 n.5
Affinity: as basis for U.S. admissions, 7, 11–12; basis for Walzerian admission policy, 11–16, 89; different from obligations, 14, 88, 116, 144; empirical evidence of, 20–21 nn.45–46; ethnic, 6–7, 11–12; family, 7–8, 12–13; ideological, 8–9, 13–16; plurality of affinities in U.S., 9, 12, 15–16, 144; with those from unjust regimes, 13–16, with Vietnamese, 13, 21 n.46. *See also* Walzer, Michael
Africans: admission to Israel, 15, 101 n.20, 137 n.48 (*see also* Falasha*); admission to U.S., 12, 19 n.37
Aleinikoff, T. Alexander: concept of community, 21 n.47, 22 n.54; on deportation, 66 n.21; on Extended Voluntary Departure, 135 n.33. *See also* Community
Allende, Salvador, 124
Ambach v. Norwick, 60
Aristotle, 4
Asylum. *See* Refugees
Attorney general, parole power, 143, 148 nn.9–12

Bach, Robert, 144. *See also* Social backgrounds of aliens; Upper class bias in admissions
Barry, Brian: critique of Rawls,

23, 29–31; trustee argument, 75; on immigration, 30–31
Basic rights, 38; liberty, 39, 44; security, 38–39; subsistence, 39–40. *See also* Shue, Henry
Basic Rights Principle (BRP), 43, 103–4; assumption of risk, 126–27; different from current U.S. policy, 88, 142–43; different from Harm Principle, 43, 85, 104, 111–12; examples of, 122–24, 125–27, 129–31; Fair Share, 104–106, 122–24, 126, 129 (*see also* Fair Share); priority of aid over admissions, 122–23, 126; threshold of need, 104. *See also* Foreign Assistance; Harm Principle
Beitz, Charles, x; critique of Rawls, 29–31; on intervention in unjust regimes, 101 n.26. *See also* Intervention; World's resources
Borders, right to control, 58, 63 n.1, 65 n.13
Brain drain, 10, 52
Briggs, Vernon, 140–41, 146, 148 n.5. *See also* Manpower goals in admission policy

Cabell v. Chavez-Salido, 61
Campbell, T. D., 81, 84. *See also* Utilitarianism
Chae Chan Ping v. U.S. (Chinese Exclusion Case), 55–57
Chaney, Elsa, 114
Chile, 124
Chinese, admission to U.S., 55–58, 63 n.3
Cistenas-Estay v. INS, 126
Cohen, Marshall, 116. *See also* Moral concerns
Combatant/noncombatant distinction, 87–92, 115–19. *See also* Harm Principle; War
Communist countries, admission from, 7, 10, 15, 20–21 nn.45–46, 115–19, 134 n.25, 143, 148–49 n.12, 149 n.17; asylum, 134 n.25; policy questioned, 143–44. *See also names of specific countries*; *see also* Ideology in U.S. alien admissions; Refugees
Community: Aleinikoff's views, 21 n.47, 22 n.54; basis for a Walzerian alien admission policy, 8–11; clash with affinity, 9–11, 14–15; disruption by refugee resettlement in U.S., 119; importance of protecting, 16, 85, 152; Rawls's concern, 24–25, 31; Walzer's views, 3–6. *See also* Walzer, Michael
Community in America: bifurcation of, 60–62; development by judiciary, 57–62; fear of alien disruption, 55–57; political exception, 60–62
Cuba, admission from, to U.S., 7, 17 n.13, 89, 133 n.13, 136 n.35, 143–44, 148 n.10; population projections, x

Deportation, judicial deference, 59, 66 n.21. *See also* Judicial deference
Developing countries: admission to U.S., 19 n.37; increased population, x; refugee flows, 37–38. *See also* Foreign assistance; Basic Rights Principle
Discrimination against aliens, 60–62. *See also* Community in America
Doppelt, Gerald, 19 n.34

Duties: Basic Rights Principle based on, 80–81, 103–4; during war, 83, 86–92; general, 80; Harm Principle based on, 80–86; of individuals, 71–77; limits of Basic Rights Principle, 104–6; Rawls's natural duty to aid, 24–25, 29, 31; Shue's theory, 40–43 (*see also* Shue); special, 80, 83, 90, 120, 132–33 n.11; supporting unjust regimes, 94–98

Duvalier, Jean-Claude (Baby Doc), 101–2 n.27, 122. *See also* Haitian migration

El Salvador, admission from, to U.S., 9, 119–21, 134 n.27, 135 nn.30–32. *See also* Harm Principle; Sanctuary

Emigration: Communist bloc, 10, 18 n.30; Haiti, 18 n.30; Walzer's view, xiv, 10–11

Ethiopian relief, 15, 72, 134 n.25, 137 n.48. *See also* Falasha; Israel, migration to

Expatriation, 64 n.11

Extended Voluntary Departure (EVD), 121, 135 n.33. *See also* El Salvador, admission from, to U.S.

Fair Share, 104–6, 122–24; examples, 122–24, 126, 129; neighbors, 123–24. *See also* Basic Rights Principle

Falasha, 15, 101 n.20, 137 n. 48. *See also* Ethiopian relief

Family reunification principle, 12–13, 20 n.40, 139–40, 141–43, 147 nn.1–2; admission under Harm Principle and Basic Rights Principle compared, 88, 142–43, 145; refugee admissions, 118–19; reforms proposed, 141–42; Shue's dilemma, 45–46 n.15; Walzer's defense of, 7, 12–13, 15

Feinberg, Joel, 80

Fiallo v. Bell, 58

Fishkin, James, 72, 74. *See also* Individuals, obligations of

Foley v. Connelie, 60

Fong Yue Ting v. U.S., x, xiv, 65 nn.12–13

Foreign assistance, 18 n.31, 34 n.27, 42; Ackerman, 52–53; Barry and Beitz, 29–31; rather than alien admissions, 37–38, 85, 105, 117–19, 122–23, 126, 127; under Basic Rights Principle, 104–5. *See also* Basic Rights Principle; Fair Share

Foreign policy, effects of, 98–99, 101–2 n.27. *See also* Harm Principle

Fried, Charles, 77 n.1

Gibney, Mark, 18 n.27, 65 n.15, 135–36 n.34

Graham v. Richardson, 60–61

Grahl-Madsen, Atle, 105–6, 107 n.3, 108 n.5, 126. *See also* Refugees

Grassmuck, George, 17 n.24

Great Britain, immigration policies of, 19 n.38

Grotius, Hugo, ix

Grounds for alien exclusion, 63 n.2, 65 n.14

Guestworker programs, x, 107 n.3

Haiti, U.S. military occupation of, 122, 136 n.41

Haitian migration, 18 n.30, 101–2 n.27, 121–24, 136 nn.41–42
Haitian Refugee Center v. Civiletti (HRC), 66 n.18, 122, 136 n.42
Hampton v. Mow Sung Wong, 61–62
Harm Principle (HP), 43, 82–98, 100 n.9, 107, 109–12, 114–22, 124–25, 127–31, 135 n.32, 137 n.45, 142–43, 145–46. *See also* Basic Rights Principle; Foreign assistance
Hart, H. L. A., 80
Helton, Arthur, 22 n.53, 134 n.25, 148–49 n.12
Higham, John, 9, 57
Hoffman, Stanley, 72–74. *See also* Individuals, obligations of
Huntington, Samuel, 104–5

Ideology, in U.S. alien admissions, 15, 22 nn.52–53, 121, 134 n.25, 143–46, 149 n.14. *See also* Communist countries; Refugees
Illegal aliens, x, 15, 62, 64 n.8, 111–14, 140. *See also* Simpson-Mazzoli legislation
Immigration and Naturalization Service (INS), 12, 19 n.37, 20 n.40; incompetence of, 132 n.6
Immigration and Naturalization Service Statistical Yearbook, 12–13, 19 n.37, 20 n.40, 136 n.36
Immigration legislation: current, 12, 20 nn. 39–40, 63 n.2, 66–67 n.23, 139; refugee legislation, 143; Simpson-Mazzoli, x, xi, xv, 45–46 n.15, 56, 113, 131–32 n.1; 1920s legislation, 11; 1965 Act, 12, 139. *See also* Simpson-Mazzoli
Individual autonomy, protection of: basis of Basic Rights Principle, 103–4; basis of Harm Principle, 79–86; basis of Rawlsian alien admission policy, 31; deficiencies in Walzer's theory, 4, 10–11, 19 nn.34–35, 95–96, 123; distinction of those singled out for persecution, 97–98; premise of Walzer's ideological affinity, 13–14; protection during war, 86–92; rationales for, 75–76, 79–80; Rawls's concern, 27–29, 33 n.21; refugees, 21 n.47; Singer's theory, 36–37; subsistence rights, 30
Individuals, obligations of: aid those in need, 24–25, 36, 71–76; alien admissions, limits to, 76; limits on, 5, 11, 32, 72–75, 81; state as agent, 71–72
Initial entry, judicial deference, 58. *See also* Judicial deference
International Labour Organization, 20 nn.42–43, 136 n.39
International law, 85–86, 88, 90–92
Intervention, in other states, 4, 10–11, 19 nn.34, 33 n.20, 35, 131; alien admissions compared, 28, 95–96, 123
Invitation to do business, 82–83; limits on nonculpability, 93–94, 128–29
Iran: admission from, to U.S., 20 n.43; complicity of U.S., 124–25; Harm Principle applied, 124–25
Israel, migration to, 15, 101 n.20, 137 n.48. *See also* Ethiopian relief

James, Susan, 74. *See also* Individuals, obligations of

Jews, admission to U.S., 17 n.15, 148 n.9
Judicial deference, 58–60, 65 n.15, 66 n.18. See also Deportation; Reentry doctrine

Karst, Kenneth, 57
Keely, Charles: on causes of refugee flows, 37; on efficiency of alien admissions, 90; on family reunification, 141, 146
Khomeini, Ayatollah, 124–25. See also Iran
King, Lawrence, 122–23, 136 n.42
King, Timothy, 135 n.32

Landon v. Plascencia, 59
Legitimate regime, definition of, 94–95. See also Unjust regime
Lichtenberg, Judith, 109–14
Lopez, Gerald, 110, 114

MacLean, Douglas, 94
Manpower goals in admission policy, 12–13, 140–41, 147 n.2
Martin, David, 18 n.29, 66 n.21, 91–91
Martinez-Romero v. INS, 135 n.32
Matthews v. Diaz, 61
Mexicans: arguments for preferred admission, 48, 109–114; naturalization rates, 64 n.5; proposal for increased admissions, 131–32 n.1
Miller, David, 80
Multinational corporations, 92–94

Nativism, in America, 55–57. See also Community in America
Naturalization rates, 64 n.5
Naverson, Jan, 137 n.44
Normal flow immigration, 12, 64 n.7, 88, 139–40

Number of aliens admitted to the U.S., 17 nn.13–18, 19 n.37, 64 n.7, 115–16, 121, 133 n.13, 148–49 n.12

Occupational preferences, 12

Philippines, admission from, to U.S., 114, 132 n.8
Pido, Antonio, 114
Pinochet, Agusto, 124
Piore, Michael, 18 n.25, 67 n.40
Plato, 4
Plyler v. Doe, 62
President's Select Commission on Immigration and Refugee Policy (SCIRP), 20 n.44, 44 n.20, 64 n.7, 67 n.40, 141–42, 148 nn.6–7, 149 n.17
Public opinion: Cuban migration, 20–21 n.45; Hungarian migration, 20 n.45; illegal aliens, 64 n.8; normal flow admissions, 64 n.8; Vietnamese, 13, 21 n.46, 64 n.8

Rawls, John: Barry-Beitz critique, 23, 29–31; on civil disobedience, 26–27; on conscription, 27–28; on difference principle worldwide, 23; on intolerant groups, 25–26, 28, 33 n.13; on militants, 25, 27; on natural duty to aid, 24–25, 29, 31; "Rawlsian" alien admission policy, 24–29; on social approbation, 28–29; two principles of justice, 32 n.2; on unjust regimes, 25, 27; on well-ordered society, 24–25, 31
Reentry doctrine, 59–60, 66 nn.22–23. See also Judicial deference

Refugees: asylum rates, 119 (Salvadorans), 121 (Haitians), 134 n.25 (Russian, Afghan, and Ethiopian applicants); critique of current definition, 91–92; family reunification, 118–19, 134 n.22, 147 n.1; persecution questioned, 143–44; public opinion, 20–21 n.45, 21 n.46, 64 n.8 (*see also* Public opinion); resettlement, 67 n.33, 90, 134 n.22; U.S. admissions, 17 nn. 13–18, 19 n.37, 133 n.13, 148–49 n.12; U.S. history, 143; Vietnamese, 115–19

Repatriation, after hostilities cease, 88–89. *See also* Harm Priniciple; War

Restitution, for harm caused, 80–85, 92–93, 111–12, 127–29; Vietnam policy, 117–19. *See also* Harm Principle; Tort law

Rosenberg v. Fleuti, 59

Rousseau, Jean-Jacques, 4–5, 31

Sanctuary movement, 9, 18 nn.26–27, 119, 121, 135–36 n.34, 144

Scanlan, John, 20 n.45, 148 n.10

Schuck, Peter, 57, 63 n.1

Shacknove, Andrew, 101 n.17

Shah of Iran, 124–25

Shue, Henry: on basic rights, 38–40; on basis for alien admissions, 38–39, 45–46 n.15; on control over multinationals, 93; on Dutch harm to Java, 41, 43, 81, 112; on duties of individuals, 72; on open-ended duties, 41–43; on protecting human life, 103; on serious harms, 83–84; on tripartite duties, 40–43

Sidgwick, Henry, 4–5

Simon, Rita, 144

Simpson-Mazzoli legislation, x, xi, xv, 45–46 n.15, 56, 113, 131–32 n.1. *See also* Immigration, legislation

Singer, Peter, 36, 74, 84

Social backgrounds of aliens, 12–13, 20 n.43, 115–16, 121, 147 n.4; different under proposed system, 88, 145–46. *See also* Upper class bias in admissions

Soviet Union, admission from, to U.S., 7, 17 n.15, 18 n.30, 149 n.17. *See also* Jews, admission to U.S.

Suhrke, Astri, 133 n.15

Teitelbaum, Michael, x, xv, 64 n.8, 99, 101–2 n.27, 133–34 n.17

Tort law: assumption of risk, 82, 99 n.6; parallel with Harm Principle, 81–83

Trustee, state as, 73, 75, 86, 92, 129, 140–41, 146

Tucker, Robert, xv, 100 n.9

United Nations High Commissioner for Refugees (UNHCR), 119, 134 nn.26–27

Unjust regime: basis of Ackerman's admission policy, 48, 52; basis of Walzer's ideological affinity, 14–15; "but for" limitation, 97, 125; differences in levels of persecution, 97–98; implication by support, 96–98, 129–30; Rawls's theory, 25–27; support for, as basis for Harm Principle, 94–98. *See also* Chile; Iran

Upper class bias in admissions: normal flow immigration, 12–

13, 20 nn.42–43, 140, 147 n.4; refugees, 115–16, 121. *See also* Social backgrounds of aliens
Utilitarianism, 36–38, 81, 84

Vattel, Emmerich, ix
Vietnamese, admission to U.S., 7, 13, 17 n.14, 89, 115–19, 133 n.14, 149 n.17; Amerasian preference, 118; public opinion, 13, 21 n.46, 64 n.8; re-education camp victims, 118
Volpe v. Smith, 66 n.22

Walzer, Michael: on admission of aliens as community decision, 8, 77 n. 10; on affinity, 6–8, 11–16; on community, 3–6, 8–11, 16 n.1; on emigration, xiv, 10–11; on family reunification, 7, 12–13, 15; on limited obligations, 5, 11, 32, 41, 81; on members-strangers, 5–7, 9–11, 14–16; on national autonomy, 4, 10, 18 n.28, 19 n.35, 95–96, 123; on neighborhoods, restricting immigration, 8–9; on protecting noncombatants, 87; rationales for alien admissions, 8–16; on social contract, 4–6; on subcommunities, 8–9. *See also* Affinity; Community
War, as basis for admission, 43, 86–92; El Salvador, 119–21; hypothetical example of Harm Principle, 125–27; reparations, 85, 100 n.8; Vietnam, 115–19
Wicclair, Mark, 33 n.20
World's resources, as morally arbitrary, 29–31; equal access versus equal use, 30–31

ABOUT THE AUTHOR

MARK GIBNEY is Assistant Professor of Political Science at Purdue University, West Lafayette, Indiana. He has published articles on alien admissions in *Boston College International and Comparative Law Review*, *Commonweal*, and *Contemporary Review*.

12.15.88